Return On
Integrity

Return On Integrity

The Individual's Journey
to the One Essential Thing

JOHN G. BLUMBERG

For ordering information or special discounts on bulk purchases please contact
Keynote Concepts, Inc. at info@BlumbergROI.com or 630-357-7897

Cover and text design by Sheila Parr
Cover image © JuliarStudio / iStockphoto

Cataloging-in-Publication data is available.
Print ISBN: 978-1-7326339-1-9

Published by Keynote Concepts, Inc.
Printed in the United States of America
First Edition

*Dedicated to all who individually dig
to collectively create integrity.*

Contents

Opening Thoughts

Six years ago, I sat on this same stone bench in the Spruce Plot of the Morton Arboretum in Lisle, Illinois, contemplating a concept. Maybe it would be more accurate if I said I had sensed the existence of a void, and I was trying to determine what the void was. It was not that I felt something was missing, something we'd once had that was no longer available to us. Rather it was something we were overlooking, and, therefore, we were not benefitting from the value it could offer us.

It wasn't about creating another solution. Even great solutions only seem to go so far, until yet another is needed. Nor was it like a resolution. It was more like a realization, an invitation. This sense didn't entail new skills, behavior modifications, stretch goals, or fulfilling a need.

The most confusing part was that it wasn't about something new. Nor was it about something unheard of. Rather it was about something *unknown*. It wasn't about something we had to go get. Oddly enough, *we already have it*. I realized that we all have something lying dormant within us, inviting us to plug into it.

This "something" is our core. More specifically, it is our core values. Our core values are not what we value. Defining core values in this way is a trap that simply leads to more empty behaviors, wants, needs, opinions, and beliefs. Our core values *are* our values.

As I sat on this rough stone bench on that cool spring day, this sense felt as overwhelming as the plethora of towering pine trees reaching over me and as far as my eyes could see. At the same time, this sense was reaching for me.

I began to scribble down what would become the "Opening Thoughts" section of my book *Return On Integrity: The New Definition of ROI and Why Leaders Need to Know It*. It took almost four years of contemplating great questions and having endless conversations to evolve those initial thoughts into a manuscript, written specifically for the leader at the top—the chairman of the board, CEO, president, executive director.

I was certain that those leaders were the linchpin to this "plug-in." First they would plug into their own core, and then they would guide the plug into the core of the organization they led, ultimately building a return on integrity—the ROI—that they needed the most. I am still certain of their responsibility.

Yet as I returned to this same stone bench six years later, I was more certain of something else. Everyone—*each and every* person—is equally the linchpin to the integrity of their own core and the core of the organization and all that flows from it.

Integrity is the fabric of the values at your core, and you are a thread of the integrity of any group you weave into: an organization, a division, a team, your family unit, or your social group. Your thread goes wherever you go. The individual contribution you make to the collective return on integrity is determined by the substance of your thread.

The pages that follow will be much more of a personal journey than an organizational strategy. Yet it will be the most strategic contribution you will ever make, moment-to-moment and day by day, in both your personal and professional lives. It will make everything else you do exponentially more valuable.

This is not a long book, nor is it a short read. You will want to experience it a little at a time. You will note suggested "pause points" along the way. You certainly will want to add your own. What's in this book is only intended to point to the one essential thing inside of you.

This integrity within you is reaching, ready to be rediscovered. Are you ready?

On the stone bench
In the Spruce Plot
At the Morton Arboretum
Lisle, Illinois

Part One

Dilemma

Sometimes we are blind to the truth.
Our blindness doesn't change the truth;
it simply creates a dilemma.

We may very well be blind to the truth when it comes to building value with core values. Maybe this is because we don't stop long enough to see the truth because of fear, intellectual arrogance, concern it may demand a change, or, at our rapid pace, it may be more convenient not to look.

Realizing a return *on* integrity first requires a return *to* integrity that will help us find the truth. We'll begin right where we are—immersed on many fronts in blindness and the dilemma our blindness creates.

I define dilemma as some of the obstacles that may stand in

the way of discovering your core values and then subsequently living them. A few of those obstacles are obvious roadblocks, and others are subtle or, like hidden land mines, imperceptible. I offer these examples to challenge you to open your eyes and look at where you may have been blinded to the truth or avoided it. These examples are simply offered for your consideration. They are not intended to stand alone as a comprehensive list; they are meant to inspire you to brainstorm and create your own list.

Some of these examples may not initially ring 100 percent factually accurate. I have included each of these ideas for consideration because I have seen where they have a very direct implication on our ability to discover our personal core values, to understand them, own them, and consistently live them.

Like someone turning on the light after being in a dark room, you may first squint reflexively. Slowly but surely, you will be able to open your eyes all the way. Once your eyes are open, your mind and eventually your heart and soul will follow. From there, an amazing opportunity can emerge. Truth doesn't change, but it will change us if we will allow it to do so.

You may be tempted to jump forward to the "Discovery" section, pick up a shovel, and start digging to your core. Doing so would present a significant level of risk, because embracing your dilemmas is the first and most important part of understanding how best to dig.

TRUTH DOESN'T CHANGE,
BUT IT WILL CHANGE US IF
WE WILL ALLOW IT TO DO SO.

DRIFT

I sat in a Chicago coffee shop on a frigid January afternoon working on the original manuscript for my book, *GOOD to the CORE*. Outside, everything seemed to be frozen in time and place. It was in this unlikely scene that I first penned these words about dilemma: "We don't go running away from our values. We go drifting away. And one day we wake up in a place we never meant to be, drifting in a direction we never would have chosen."

We've all experienced drift. But many of us have probably never opened our eyes to the danger of how something so subtle could lead us down a road to something so tragic. Show me a corporation, association, politician, athletic program, religious institution, or marriage where there has been an implosion, and I will show you where there has been a breakdown at the core. The breakdown didn't happen overnight. *It happened over time.*

Breakdowns are surprising when they happen, especially when the apex of the problem rests on the shoulders of smart, experienced, successful people. In most cases, it rests with people who have worked incredibly hard to arrive at what is at once the height of their success and the precipice of their fall.

I don't know about you, but I don't run into that many people who say they *don't* want to operate from a set of core values. How then do we have so many breakdowns at the core with all of these good people at the helm?

The drift may be the most dangerous dilemma of all. The drift is subtle, and subtle is hard to detect. Though not necessarily

WE DON'T GO RUNNING AWAY FROM OUR VALUES. WE GO DRIFTING AWAY. AND ONE DAY WE WAKE UP IN A PLACE WE NEVER MEANT TO BE, DRIFTING IN A DIRECTION WE NEVER WOULD HAVE CHOSEN.

invisible to others, our own drift often is invisible to us. Knowing your core values doesn't prevent you from drifting. In fact, you can pretty much be sure you will begin to drift while facing daily demands, challenging relationships, and the reality of your humanity. But if you know where you started, *you will know when you have left.* When you start to drift, knowing your core values will let you know you have left your core. Your core values are like a microscope, magnifying what is incapable of being seen by the naked eye.

The drift rarely begins with a major decision. Like water, it will find the path of least resistance. It creeps its way into seemingly insignificant, simple daily decisions. It comes when we are in a rush, when bigger things are pressing.

The path to questionable needs, wants, choices, and behaviors is typically not a short one. It is seductively incremental, likely undetectable, and paved with some magnetic temptations. The greatest loss of all may be the diminished potential you experience when unplugged from your core. It serves us well to know the very moment we leave.

I think we would be shocked to see how many little decisions made each day can trigger drift. But it isn't about paying attention to each and every decision. It's about investing in what intentionally informs those decisions for you, whether those decisions are personal or organizational.

NEW VENEER

Core values seem to be talked about, tossed about, and taped to corporate walls at an increasing rate. On the surface, that would appear to be a great thing. Unless, of course they stay there—on the surface.

My fear is that core values have become the latest widespread veneer. Veneers are specifically designed to make something look like what it's not. Veneers work well on furniture but not on the core of our personal and professional lives. If we think about and discuss core values in only a shallow way, we are simply applying a veneer. Values hold little value unless they flow from deep within your core.

When core values are used as a veneer, they can clearly cause more harm than good.

ASSUMPTIONS

You will find there are many challenges when it comes to the topic of core values. Paradoxically, I find many of these challenges inspire an individual to keep digging. But there is one challenge that predictably will keep someone from ever picking up their shovel. It is called assumption.

One of the most subtle and dangerous dilemmas we face when it comes to core values is our assumptions, especially assumptions we make about the concept of core values itself. Intellectually, it is not a hard concept to grasp. In today's workplace, where we have access to endless sophisticated personal-development books, podcasts, and assessments, the concept of core values can seem almost overly simplistic. It's easy to quickly check the concept off the list as all figured out and fully understood.

There is also another widespread assumption at play. Over a number of years, we have done a great disservice to the concept of core values. We have made them soft, touchy-feely wall coverings we turn to when it's convenient. They're the topics of discussion at management retreats and the sweet side of a tough business world.

There's nothing touchy-feely or sweet about core values. They form the backbone of every individual who chooses to have one. Core values aren't about making nice, easy decisions. Nor are they your excuse to avoid tough decisions. They are your asset in every decision you make, and they bring their greatest value when the decisions are the toughest. Nice decisions are for short-term convenience and have no grounding in core values. Hard decisions, made through the context of core values, will get you to the right decision in a credible way.

The biggest risk, however, is assuming we actually know what our own core values are. A presumptive assumption is a roadblock and for some a dangerous dead end. This is true in numerous aspects of our work, relationships, faith, and professional development. This is especially true when it comes to digging to our core. Assuming we know what our core values are can stop the process before it has begun. I'm reminded of Anthony de Mello's focus on the importance of unlearning. What we assume we "know" may be the very thing we need to unlearn to open the door to discovery. My hope is that you will be digging deeper than you ever thought possible, well beyond all that you have unknowingly assumed.

The only approach to this dilemma is to take a second look. In fact, the whole concept of building value with core values is unique precisely because you have to look at it again and again and again. Core values demand your full attention.

EXCUSES

It is convenient to see core values as just another thing rather than the *main* thing of everything. It is always easier to write off something as insignificant or assume it won't make a meaningful difference. Doing so allows us to move on to the next item on our list—something "worthy" of our attention. We don't have to do anything further about it.

Moving on feels especially justified if we have repeatedly experienced flavor-of-the-month after flavor-of-the-month initiatives in our workplace, especially when those initiatives have been about temporary leadership nods to organizational core values.

Writing off digging for core values won't demand anything from you in the short run, yet it may take everything from you in the long term.

WRITING OFF DIGGING FOR CORE VALUES WON'T DEMAND ANYTHING FROM YOU IN THE SHORT RUN, YET IT MAY TAKE EVERYTHING FROM YOU IN THE LONG TERM.

GENERATIONS

Never before have so many generations been simultaneously in the active workforce. Some would estimate that today's workforce spans four or five generations. It seems an entire industry of consultants, speakers, and books has been focused on the differences among these generations. Many important insights have surfaced from the examination of these differences.

The dilemma here isn't the generations. The dilemma is our dwelling on their surface-level differences without digging deeper. Generations, by definition, are lumped into generalizations, and generalizations have a way of pulling us to the surface. When you combine the dwelling on differences with the absence of an intentional awareness of personal core values, you create an even greater divide among generations.

This is true in all aspects of diversity: cultures, genders and gender orientation, ethnicity, and deeply seated differences in opinions and beliefs. Staying on the surface of anything or anyone will always lead you to a set of differences, disconnects, and unhealthy divides—especially when that is what you're looking for.

I think we would be surprised to find that the deeper we dig into the core values of individuals among any different grouping, the more we might find how much they have in common. Starting with what is different between individuals takes you on a very different path than first digging for what they deeply have in common at their core.

STARTING WITH WHAT IS DIFFERENT BETWEEN INDIVIDUALS TAKES YOU ON A VERY DIFFERENT PATH THAN FIRST DIGGING FOR WHAT THEY DEEPLY HAVE IN COMMON AT THEIR CORE.

RELIGIOUS MYTH

Some people will push back on focusing on core values because they feel core values might be a bit religious in nature. On the other hand, I find that those deeply grounded in their religion have just as much trouble discovering their core values as anyone else. Values are about deep convictions, but they are different from a theology.

Consider this: If core values were religious, fewer religious institutions would have the same human struggles as secular organizations. Why do faithful individuals have the same human struggles as individuals who claim no faith at all? A religious person would be as well served as a nonreligious person to journey the same pathway to personal and organizational core values. It may very well help them deepen their faith and more deeply live the faith they have. All individuals may find it to be a deeply spiritual experience.

Pause Point

- When was there a season or specific circumstance in your own life where you drifted? How was that experience for you? How subtle was your drift? When did you (or others) first notice your drift? What do you perceive was the cost—and more importantly—the lost potential because of your drift? What did you learn then, and how might it inform your experience today?

- How have you personally experienced core values as a veneer—and where have you made your own assumptions or excuses?

- Where do you potentially experience your own surface-level misunderstandings with cases of different generations, gender issues, race, nationalities, religion, or with anyone who has had different experiences or current circumstances than you?

PERCEPTION DECEPTION

Perception is a powerful force. It stems from perspective, and perspective is often driven by our prior experiences and current circumstances. These certainly can alter what we see and how we feel. They can lead us to some factual conclusions about our experience and to some unfounded assumptions, too.

Not to oversimplify, but I often think about how the temperature on any given day can be a great indicator of my theory. A 45-degree day is factually a 45-degree day, no matter when it occurs. But the 45-degree autumn day may feel downright cold, while the 45-degree winter day can embrace us with a sense of warmth. The same set of facts viewed from a different perspective can create a completely different perception.

This truth doesn't only apply to temperatures. If it goes unnoticed, it can prove fatal to all of us—especially those of us without a well-defined core. The problem is that sometimes it is so unnoticeable . . . unless we are consciously aware that perception deception is continually in play. We all need a strategic counterattack to diminish the blinding capability of this deception.

Sometimes this deception can be fed from the outside, when we surround ourselves only with people who think like we do and have precisely the same viewpoints—whether on business strategy, politics, spiritual practices, or theological beliefs. When you never have a counterpoint, you can rest assured it's only a matter of time until you are well on your way to drifting toward the deception of your own perception.

Counter viewpoints don't have to change our stance, but they do need to test our perception. More often than not, they will fine-tune our stance.

The way to easily see the blinding impact of circumstances is to realize how quickly we see a perception deception in others. We are not in their circumstances. We don't share their blind spots. We can, therefore, see their missteps, their drift in motion. Unless, of course, we are looking through our own perception deception rather than from our core.

BLIND PASSION

Like all things, passion can have its dark side. We can get caught up in the momentum that our passion creates. It's been spoken about in numerous ways. I like to think about it in terms of the old wisdom of "see no evil, hear no evil, speak no evil." Detached from a defined set of core values, our passion can seed a revised version of this old Eastern wisdom. Initially intended to inspire no association with evil, the Western adaption of this speaks to the risk of turning a blind eye to the darker side of our passions.

You could describe this as the ends justifying the means. But it's different than that. The ends justifying the means is a bit of an intentional justification. This is more subtle and fully unintentional. Much like the drift, you are blinded by its tightening grip.

Our passion is a beautiful thing when fueled from a well-defined core. Values must precede passion. Otherwise passion can curdle values into poison. Where core values precede passion, they are woven into the substance of the passion. Values are the thermostat that shuts down all systems when passion begins to overheat. Otherwise passion becomes opaque within us and can eventually create a blind spot in all we see and, ultimately, in all we don't see.

Sometimes our blind spots can become our convenient coping mechanism. It's not that we can't see; it's that we choose not to see. In some cases, we look away, and in others we simply choose not to open our eyes. This often happens when we have a great position we don't want to lose. This can be in the form of a

VALUES ARE THE
THERMOSTAT THAT SHUTS
DOWN ALL SYSTEMS
WHEN PASSION BEGINS
TO OVERHEAT.

title, community stature, or even broader fame, income, or perceived self-worth. It can also happen when we choose to blindly follow a leader. We can learn to justify anything if it helps us cope. Unfortunately, the longer it goes on, the easier the medicine goes down.

SELF-IDENTITY AND ATTACHMENTS

When was the last time someone you were first meeting asked, "*Who* are you?" It's likely you haven't initially posed that question to others either. The question usually posed is, So, *what* do you do?

The problem comes when your self-identity is attached to the "what" rather than defined by the "who." The point isn't that people don't ask, "*Who* are you?" The bigger issue is, could you answer that question if they did?

Identity placed anywhere other than within our core is a pathway to attachment. It's a setup for something to lose. A person who doesn't intentionally and consciously know their own core will find their self-identity in *something* outside their core, and most likely, they will attach themselves to it.

Perhaps our best shot at remaining connected to our core is to embrace the practice of detachment from life's trappings. The things you attach to are not the problem. It is the attachment itself that begins to change the relationship you have with the trappings. At some point you no longer own them—they own you and the core within you.

The moment you attach to something, you have something to lose. We all do it to some degree. It eventually becomes a problem when you feel like you have too much to lose. By the time you realize it, you have drifted a long way from your core. As attachments cling to you, they pull you in whatever direction they need to go, and you simply follow, serving them in any way that keeps you connected to them. By that point, you have arrived at a place you never meant to be, drifting in a direction you never would have chosen.

THE THINGS YOU ATTACH TO
ARE NOT THE PROBLEM. IT
IS THE ATTACHMENT ITSELF
THAT BEGINS TO CHANGE THE
RELATIONSHIP YOU HAVE WITH
THE TRAPPINGS.

BOTTOM LINE

Some would suggest that when it comes to core values in an organization, the financial bottom line is the elephant in the room—the dilemma that creates all other dilemmas.

Some executives may believe this bottom line is the only real core value of their organization in the marketplace. And in a number of cases, it would surely appear that way. But executives aren't the only ones who believe that the bottom line is a core value. An organization might also include cynical employees who further the assertion that executives value only the bottom line. Often, it is these employees who embrace this perspective to release themselves from the responsibility of knowing and living the stated core values of the organization. Doing so takes them off the hook for a lot of personal accountability. It can be a very convenient perspective and excuse.

This dilemma also shows up in a desire for endless wealth accumulation in private households. Whether it is at work or at home, the financial bottom line is an area where many perceptions are formed, and many motives can become questionable. In the absence of a pointed conversation and understanding concerning this issue, there is no question that the financial bottom line can become the default core value—whether we intend it to be or not.

There is a different condition at a personal or organizational bottom line that can create its own dilemma. Tough economic conditions can create a sole focus on survival, especially in the absence of a defined core. That focus on survival creates a scarcity mindset and leads ultimately to isolation and silo-minded thinking. It ignites shortsighted decisions that have very real long-term impacts.

On the other hand, if defined core values are strong, the worst economic challenges turn into opportunities for development and creativity. An even stronger individual will emerge on the other side of the storm.

Core values give purpose and meaning to everyone in an organization and in their personal lives. They're consistent reminders that all the blood, sweat, and tears spent in the fight to survive were worth it. Personal income and organizational profit are good things, and they are necessary if you want to keep your dream, mission, and vision fully alive. *But they are not core values.*

Our attention to personal income and an organization's bottom line is important. But obsession with either eventually becomes the enemy of core values. In fact, it often encourages and enables behavior that undermines core values. Ultimately, this obsession defines its own set of core values, and a deadly partnership is formed.

It might be helpful to think of personal income and organizational profit to be like sleep. Sleep is critical to the functioning of the brain. It impacts memory, critical-thinking skills, and your ability to think creatively. Sleep allows the brain to process, sort, and store information for retrieval at a later point.

But as important as sleep is to the functioning of the brain,

AN EVEN STRONGER
INDIVIDUAL WILL EMERGE
ON THE OTHER SIDE
OF THE STORM.

we don't live to sleep. In fact, too much sleep would eventually diminish and destroy the very thing it is designed to support—the health of the very core of your body. Muscles would become weak, breathing would become shallow, and vital organs would begin to shut down. The same is true for personal income and organizational profit. It is a bit of a paradox. Something so critical to funding and keeping personal goals and the dream of an organization alive is the very thing that will destroy a household or an organization if it becomes the be-all and end-all—if it becomes a core value.

GREED

Greed knows no economic or demographic boundary. In the economic boom of the 1990s, *Fast Company* magazine tucked a powerful question into the lower corner of the cover of a monthly issue. It asked, *When is enough, enough?* It is an important question that few people take the time to answer. It sounds limiting, but, paradoxically, answering it is quite empowering. It's a matter of richness rather than riches.

Success is a wonderful thing. Yet what you do with your success is certainly influenced by the answer to that simple question: When is enough, enough? No one, generally, decides to embrace greed. We are typically blind to it, and it is blinding to us. It is especially blinding when it comes to our core.

Greed is very different from reaping the rewards of our lifetime of effort and results. Rewards can motivate us. Greed changes our motives.

Over time, greed redefines our core. When we are not connected to our core, it is only a matter of time until our core becomes connected to something else.

Asking the question *When is enough, enough?* isn't about creating limitations. It is about establishing a grounded perspective. Individuals can't simply decide they are not going to fall prey to greed. They have to protect themselves with a deep sense of their own personal values, and these personal values must intersect with the values of the organization where they work. They must make a relentless commitment to live those values each and every day.

It can be a terrifying experience to face your core—to find out who you really are—when you have become someone different from the person you hoped to be.

WHEN IS ENOUGH, ENOUGH?

Pause Point

- When was there a time where your passion was so great that you risked being blinded to the truth because of choice, convenience, fear, or loss?

- What do you hold so tightly (e.g., circumstances, possessions, relationships, security, beliefs, opinions, grudges, traditions, fear, wants, needs, behaviors, or otherwise) that it may very well have become an attachment for you?

- Is your own financial bottom line a core need or a core value? How does that drive you or impact you? How much thought have you given to when is enough, enough?

FEAR OF FAILURE . . . AND SUCCESS

We all would be well served to assess our fears. Not acknowledging them can have significant implications in our day-to-day perspectives and behaviors.

My great friend and leadership expert Kevin Freiberg first drew my attention to this powerful question: Are you playing to win—or playing not to lose? Fear of failure will always put you in a defensive posture of playing *not to lose*. It is a weak and boring approach to life.

While playing not to lose can feel like a secure approach, it may very well be a deceptive wedge driven between an individual and their core.

On the other hand, success can create its own demands. Henry Kissinger, the fifty-sixth US secretary of state, put it this way: "Each success only buys you a ticket to a more difficult problem."

This is true. Few of us can escape the incremental demands of continued success. The increasing demands could be the most conscious or subconscious fear of all. Most of us won't necessarily see it as a fear of success, but we will likely feel the fear of the demands success brings. The increasing demands can bring the dawning of a drift from your core. Intentionally trying to eliminate fear can be a tall order. Your willingness to embrace your core can eventually make the fear irrelevant. You might say it is one of the returns on integrity.

FEAR OF FAILURE WILL
ALWAYS PUT YOU IN A
DEFENSIVE POSTURE OF
PLAYING NOT TO LOSE.

ERUPTION OF DISRUPTION

There was a time when change evolved quite slowly. I'm sure the turtle pace of change didn't seem as such at the time. These historical changes typically reflected a modified version of the old—a new model of what already existed. Today we live a whole different pace of change. And we are in slow motion compared to where we are headed—toward outright disruption.

Disruption isn't change. Disruption erases the old with something completely new. Sometimes disruption is about doing things in new ways, but real disruption is about seeing things in completely different ways. The "new way of doing" is merely the by-product of this disrupted insight. Amid disruption, a refresh of most anything—a repackaging of the old—brings little value. This refresh feels like progress, but it nurtures the behaviors for falling further behind. The long-overused cliché of rearranging the chairs on the *Titanic* captures this.

Disruption may not only create a new context of how we live today, it can also help us rethink how individuals and organizations approach discovering their core. Disruption involves looking out, looking around, and most importantly, looking individually within. Disruption can be delightfully uncomfortable and sometimes acutely painful. If it is not, you can be sure you are refreshing an old way of being and not in the midst of disruption.

The perception of ourselves and our workplace culture are temporarily changed with a forced set of new behaviors. On the other hand, our reality is forever disrupted when we are willing to dig much deeper than we ever thought possible, to see meaningful personal and organizational values that we never knew existed. These values are unshaken by the most profound external disruptions and quite often fuel them. They also fuel a meaningful disruption in how we see ourselves and workplace culture to begin with.

The exponential speed of future external disruptions won't encourage personal and organizational core values. It will demand them!

ARE YOU UP FOR A CRISIS?

Victor H. Mair, a Chinese philologist at the University of Pennsylvania, corrects what he says is a long-standing popular misinterpretation of the Chinese word for "crisis." It is often mentioned as the symbols noting *danger* plus *opportunity*. He notes that the portion interpreted as *danger* (or *precarious*) is accurate, but the portion often referred to as *opportunity* would be more accurately described as *critical point*.

Without an intentionally grounded and frequently visited set of personal and organizational core values, a crisis is certainly a dangerously critical point. It is also a terrible time to try to determine your core values. However, when grounded in a set of core values, every crisis is an opportunity to further deepen your understanding and commitment to those values.

SOCIAL MEDIA

Technology always comes packaged as an enhancement, a leap forward in efficiency and productivity. And very often it is just that. Social media can create the opportunity for connections. It can open the door to new relationships, both near and incredibly far away.

But, by definition, what social media does is create a context for developing shallow connections. In many cases, the environment it promotes is one of transactional relationships. It can eventually train us to operate solely on a surface level, not only with others but with ourselves as well. A plethora of shallow connections, an endless deluge of quick sound bites, and an ever-accelerating pace can push us stealthily to live on the surface of relationships, thoughts, and feelings. It can also coerce us to live in a place increasingly distant from our core.

There is no stopping technology, which is precisely why personal core values and the core values of communities of people who make up organizations will only become all the more important. Otherwise social media creates an ever-increasing dilemma.

MEASUREMENTS AND REWARDS

The majority of measurements in organizations are designed to deliver the "what" an organization wants or needs, and this is most often tied to production and productivity. Most types of measurements are designed to drive intended outcomes and inspire behavior—whether by motivation or by fear. This is also true when it comes to personal goals we set for ourselves. The goals certainly engage their own version of accountability. But they can also drive unintended outcomes and consequences. Often these consequences are the result of measurements that induce behaviors in direct or indirect violation of specific stated or intended organizational or personal core values.

It is important to realize that everything is systemic whether it is intentionally integrated or not.

I do believe measurements and goals are vitally important. You are more likely to achieve something if you establish a measure for it. The problem arises when you get unintended consequences that you don't plan for. In the absence of a deep connection to core values, the "how" in which you achieve the measurement becomes fair game, and the consequences, intended or not, eventually become destructive. You want core values to steer the measurement process from the very beginning, not the other way around.

With that said, the biggest dilemma of measurement today may have nothing to do with what or how you measure. It has more to do with the fact that the most important things may not be quantifiably measurable by a computer at all.

YOU WANT CORE VALUES TO STEER THE MEASUREMENT PROCESS FROM THE VERY BEGINNING, NOT THE OTHER WAY AROUND.

A new year always offers the opportunity for a new beginning. Research shows that a high percentage of New Year's resolutions have already gone by the wayside just five days into the new year. I quit making New Year's resolutions long ago, because I fell into this gone-by-the-wayside percentage far too often. This high percentage begs the question: Why don't these resolutions stick?

For some people, New Year's resolutions mark an attempt at some form of improvement around a specific behavior. That can be a positive thing indeed. Yet, like many workplace-improvement initiatives, they can be random and disconnected. Often, New Year's resolutions are reactive rather than responsive to something much deeper and intentional.

Rather than starting or stopping a specific behavior, maybe it's time to pick up a shovel and start digging for something deeper, richer, and more systemically connected to real transformation. Before you pick up your shovel, it might be fair warning to know the following about your dig:

- It takes longer than you expect.
- It seems simple and straightforward until it gets very confusing and elusive.
- There will be incredible resistance from within and from without.
- Other good things will distract you.
- There is no efficiency, only effectiveness.
- Vision isn't about where you're headed; it's about how you see everything more clearly through your values.

Pause Point

- In your current personal and professional circumstances, which of these dilemmas speak most to you in making it difficult to discover and/or live your personal core values?

- What other dilemmas have you experienced or are you currently experiencing that are important for you to note as roadblocks to discovering and/or living your personal core values?

Even with some great insight about various dilemmas, you may still be wondering, how do I even start to dig to my core? It's a great question. Let's go discover!

Part Two

Discovery

*Grasping for framework
while searching for perspective*

C ore values seem like a simple concept, yet nothing could be further from the truth. Discovering your core values can become confusing quite quickly. One of my greatest fears in speaking about core values was thinking that many participants were going to write off the topic as something they already knew all about. Yet, invariably, once participants start down the path of thinking beyond the surface level of the topic, the most common question I'm asked is, "What, exactly, is a core value?"

When it comes to core values, a concise definition can never explain what your individual journey will help you discover.

Along the way, levels of understanding will ebb and flow, and then in the midst of the confusion, you'll find an advanced level of clarity.

I have found a few verbose attempts to put arms around the definition of personal and organizational core values. One simple definition of "core" caught my attention: *the central, innermost, or most essential part . . . of anything.* I think it is helpful to change the last word to "anyone."

There are no words that do justice to the insights you will eventually experience along the journey of discovering your core values. No definition will ever fully guide or substitute for what you will explore, learn, and realize as you start the process of looking for what values reside within your core. You will know them when you see them, and no definition should stand as judge to them.

The mission isn't to figure out the definition of core values. The mission is to discover the values at your core. You don't exactly need the former to find the latter. The first is an intellectual exercise, and the second is an emotional awakening.

Our core and our soul could very well be described as two sides of the same coin. If so, it would be a coin that holds great value when well spent.

More pragmatically, think of your core as a kaleidoscope. With a kaleidoscope there are a few basic ingredients through which you can see a variety of beautiful designs. Yet, over time, the wide variety of designs tend to become familiar.

THE MISSION ISN'T TO
FIGURE OUT THE DEFINITION
OF CORE VALUES.
THE MISSION IS TO DISCOVER
THE VALUES AT YOUR CORE.

The process for discovering your own core will be as much of an art as it is a science. It is far more complicated, challenging, and refreshing than picking some words from a list or a few cards from a deck. This process isn't about getting to a quick answer. It's about embarking on an impactful process.

A LENS WORTH LOOKING THROUGH

More points of data, more images—and one could even argue—more insights are put before us today than ever before. In so many ways we have incredible resources at our disposal, but there are certainly downsides to the volume. A fair amount of these resources is delivered with bias or premeditated motives. Some would say the plethora of negative news has its own impact. So does the lens through which you see it.

I don't take my vision for granted. After two detached retinas (one in 2004 and the other in 2010), I have a deep gratitude for my vision each day. I certainly learned the importance of the retina. I also learned the importance of the lens through which we see. Many patients who undergo retinal reattachment quickly find themselves back in surgery months later, not for the retina but for the lens in front of it. Cataract surgery is a common procedure in the months following a retinal reattachment. The surgeon actually removes and replaces the eye's lens. It's an amazing process that significantly enhances vision almost immediately.

As a cataract ripens, it clouds your vision. External intervention, such as glasses or contacts, will eventually no longer help. The only thing that can make your vision clear again is cataract surgery, replacing the lens itself.

Intentionally discovering your core values is like cataract surgery. Consider it like a lens replacement! I have come to understand core values as the lens that focuses our experiences. Values bring clarity. The question we need to ask is how clear is our lens?

Values are the lens that creates your vision—how you see the world.

GETTING THE WHOLE PICTURE OF INTEGRITY

It's not uncommon to see the word "integrity" on an individual's or organization's list of core values. I understand why people may feel compelled to include it, but I have come to see and believe that integrity is not a core value. Integrity is the fabric of every core value. This may explain why some leaders are so passionate to include it on their list. I certainly have no problem with it being on the list. It can serve as a great reminder there.

Think of integrity as a thread. The thread can be made of different substances. It could be cotton or silk or nylon. Perhaps it is wool or linen. It could be coarse or soft, thick or thin. It could become a shirt or pants or a scarf. The quality of what is created fully depends on the quality of the fabric. And the fabric is only as good as the thread that makes it. So it goes with integrity.

Integrity is not about naming a value; it's about living each of the values we have named. Integrity is about integration. It is the thread that weaves the values we have named into every relationship, every meeting, every conversation, every initiative, every measurement, every reward—everything! Integrity is what makes each individual value and the collective nature of those values that we espouse actually valuable. Without integrity, there are no core values.

INTEGRITY IS THE FABRIC
OF EVERY CORE VALUE.

GOING BLANK

People often share that as they try to think of words to describe their core values, they go blank. It's actually a wonderful place to start. We often have to let go of assumptions we have made along the way to discover what is genuine, authentic, real, and true. There is a lot of merit to beginning the process of discovering— or rediscovering—one's core values with a blank canvas.

A blank sheet of paper has a way of opening your eyes as you try to draw words from within to form your list of core values. It can be a humbling experience in coming to grips with how well you know your core. It can also be a powerful moment of inspiration to once and for all become committed to naming what lies within.

You might want to choose a nice sheet of paper, because it may end up being something you'll want to keep as a treasure for the remainder of your days. And that's not because it's the sheet where you completed the discovery of your core values, rather because it's the sheet where you started it.

Leave your phone and laptop behind and take the paper to a quiet area and sit with it alone for thirty minutes. During this time, brainstorm any idea you think you might name as a core value. Write down every word that comes to mind without filtering, criticizing, or prioritizing. Keep your pencil moving; you're going for quantity, not quality.

If you get stuck during that initial thirty-minute window or you draw a blank and your pencil stops moving, just know that

THERE IS A LOT OF MERIT TO
BEGINNING THE PROCESS OF
DISCOVERING—
OR REDISCOVERING—
ONE'S CORE VALUES WITH
A BLANK CANVAS.

it's all part of the gift of the blank sheet of paper. Embrace it, own it, and know you are simply having a really bad case of normal!

Once you have completed this exercise, do not open this book for the next three days. Each of those three days, find another ten minutes a day to review your brainstorm list and add any other words that come to mind. That's another thirty minutes across these three days. At the end of those three days, pick up where you left off reading this book!

Pause Point

- What was the "Blank Sheet of Paper" experience like for you? What surprised you? What did you notice about yourself as you initially tried to brainstorm some ideas?

- As you continued brainstorming words, what frustrated or challenged you most?

- Before your "Blank Sheet of Paper" experience, what would best describe your own perception of your connection to your core: a) you are value-based, b) you have a gut feel or intuition about your values, or c) you have an intentional understanding of specific personal values at your core? How has your "Blank Sheet of Paper" experience changed and/or informed your perception?

DIGGING YOUR WELL

Ever since I can remember, I've had a love for water fountains. In the second grade, I decided I was going to build one in our backyard. I saved my money to buy a long hose, a nozzle, bricks, Sakrete for making the concrete base, and flowers. It was my first real experience at digging.

It was a fairly basic design. I planned to hook the end of the hose to the outdoor water faucet at the back of the house and bury the hose under the ground all the way from the faucet to my perfectly conceived location for the water fountain.

The fountain design would feature an eighteen-inch by eighteen-inch cement center made with the Sakrete. I would build a wood mold for pouring the three-inch deep cement square. The trench, with the hose, would end just under where the cement square would be poured. I would attach the nozzle to the end of the hose and then anchor the nozzle, pointing straight up. Once the cement was poured, the tip of the nozzle would stick out about an inch above the level of the cement. Outside the eighteen-inch square, I would dig another twelve inches on all sides to create a flowerbed frame around the cement square. I would then frame the flowerbed with bricks. And then, of course, I would plant a bunch of bright yellow and orange marigolds. It seemed like a perfect plan.

The first challenge, as you might imagine, was getting my mom and dad to say yes. I still can't believe they agreed; my own children would tell you I would have never allowed this to happen at our house. The second challenge was digging the trench for the hose. It took a lot of digging!

I thought I would finish the entire project in one day. By sundown on that first day, I had almost finished. Well, almost finished digging the trench! I woke up in the middle of the night from the throbbing pain in the blisters in the center palm of both hands, thinking that I still had to dig out the entire area for the fountain itself.

Digging was much harder and took much longer than I ever imagined. I think it's precisely the experience we face when trying to discover our own core values. It takes a lot of digging, and it will likely take a lot longer than you expect.

Digging for your personal core values is like digging a hundred-foot-deep water well. The first thing you need to realize is that the water is there, whether you choose to dig for it or not. Without digging, of course, you won't benefit from the value there. But digging is really hard work. And it can get confusing and discouraging along the way. You dig five feet and you are still looking at dirt. You get to thirty-five feet, and you are still looking at dirt. At seventy-five feet you may be looking at rock. It's important to realize from the beginning that there will be more digging, dirt, and rock than you will anticipate. Finally, at a hundred feet you see water. It is there that you tap into the fuel of your integrity.

Digging is always a choice. It seems to be a harder choice than I first realized it would be. Staying with it seems to be even harder. I remember the palms of my little second-grade hands were starting to be really sore as I would look back and forth from the location of the faucet and the desired location of the fountain. At least I could see the distance in between and how much farther I had to go. We don't always know how much farther we need to dig to reach the well of our values. We have to just keep digging. The well is waiting within.

I have employed the simple "blank sheet of paper" experience with thousands of participants in hundreds of keynote presentations. Because of time constraints, I give three minutes for their brainstorming. That's usually all that is needed to create a wake-up call.

Over a period of two years, with audience permission, I compiled a cumulative list of the ideas they discovered during their "blank sheet of paper" experience. Their combined list is composed of behaviors, wants, needs, and, of course, some core values. I have never edited or prioritized this list. Except for exact duplications, whatever was turned in remains and is presented in alphabetical order.

As a next step, I offer you this Core Values Brainstorming List online at BlumbergROI.com/TheBigDig as a way to exponentially expand your own brainstorming of ideas—more importantly, to stir your thinking.

I would recommend printing out the Core Values Brainstorming List. It is helpful to engage with the list. Slowly read the words, letting each sink in to help trigger your own words. Circle,

THE FIRST THING YOU
NEED TO REALIZE IS THAT
THE WATER IS THERE,
WHETHER YOU CHOOSE
TO DIG FOR IT OR NOT.

underline, or highlight any words that resonate. Note whatever words of your own that come to mind. As you think about each word, try to distinguish it as a behavior, want, need, or core value. Mark each one as such. There is no right or wrong answer, but an awareness or a pattern will begin to emerge for you.

I recommend regularly returning to this brainstorming stage for a period of time—as little as a month, but possibly as much as three. As you brainstorm, keep reading. You will eventually develop an internal barometer indicating how your personal big dig is progressing and move to creating your Version 1.0 list of core values.

FLOW MATTERS

The direction of flow matters. In Chicago's early years, the Chicago River held a significant amount of sewage and factory waste. Time and time again heavy rains caused the river to swell, and the polluted waters flowed into Lake Michigan—the source of drinking water for the surrounding communities. A tragic percentage of the population was killed by illnesses caused from the contaminated water supply.

Everyone understood that the problem was not the actual source of the drinking water. That source was an incredible gift. The problem was the direction of the polluted flow of the Chicago River into that source.

Despite the doubts of most of the city's population, engineers and numerous city leaders knew the flow could be reversed. What they also knew was that it would take an investment. They knew resources were going to be required in a time of community bankruptcies and a dearth of creativity and courage. In the decades it took to gather courageous leadership, thousands continued to die from the contaminated water.

In 1900, the flow of the river was reversed. The problem was solved. While there continued to be polluted elements in the river, the contaminated water never made it into Lake Michigan. The drinking supply remained pure, and water began to flow from Lake Michigan into the Chicago River. Over the years, the reverse flow inspired a change in behaviors toward the introduction of pollution into the river itself.

As with the Chicago River, the direction of flow matters when it comes to core values. Think of our behaviors, wants, needs, and values as a systemic continuum that flows in one direction or the other. In the illustration below, the source of an unhealthy flow is behavior-driven. Along the way, well-intentioned, performance-driven behaviors are intermingled with ungrounded wants and needs, eventually flowing into a pool of unintentional core values.

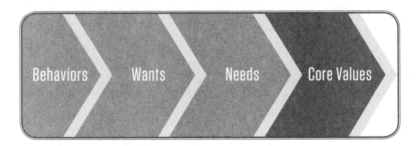

Like Lake Michigan, our core values have the potential to provide a source for living when they are intentionally chosen. However, when left unintended, the flow begins with behaviors, and eventually our core values become an unintentional, polluted catchall.

After witnessing thousands of people attempting to name their own core values through the "blank sheet of paper" experience, it's clear that most people don't have a lot of clarity when it comes to knowing their specific core values. Do they believe they are values-based? Likely. Do they have a gut feeling or an intuition? Possibly. Do they have details? Rarely. What is even less clear is distinguishing between behaviors, wants, needs, and core values, along with understanding the importance of doing so. This will be one of the most important nuances we will explore.

Our behaviors are often influenced by unfiltered pollutants. These pollutants are often made up of to-do lists, metrics, measurements, expectations in relationships, veneers to be polished, brands to be created, and messages to be spun—all eventually contaminated when they are not grounded in an intentional set of personal and organizational core values from the start.

Our wants and needs become intermingled in the turbulent flow of our rushing schedules. In the rush of this unhealthy flow, we end up *needing what we want instead of wanting what we need.* That's what happens when our flow is moving in the wrong direction.

It's especially a problem when all of this mess is pouring into what was intended to be the source—our core values. Not instantly, but eventually, our values become polluted.

Remember—it's called drift. We need to reverse the flow.

IN THE RUSH OF THIS
UNHEALTHY FLOW,
WE END UP NEEDING
WHAT WE WANT INSTEAD OF
WANTING WHAT WE NEED.

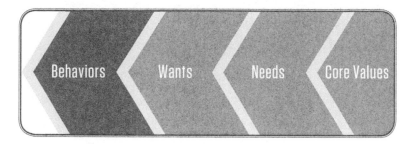

Intentionally identifying our core values is the first and most important step in reversing the flow. In doing so, our defined core values enhance the value of everything they flow into.

DISTINGUISHING BEHAVIORS, WANTS, NEEDS, AND CORE VALUES

After a thorough review of the Core Values Brainstorming List and a period of continued brainstorming, it will be time to officially start your own Version 1.0 list. It is helpful to build your list by making entries under each of the following four categories: Core Values, Needs, Wants, and Behaviors. You may want to set up these four columns in an electronic spreadsheet (e.g., Excel) so you can, with just a few keystrokes, easily move things about. You can download a template of this worksheet at BlumbergROI.com/TheBigDig. Others will prefer a real sheet of paper and a pencil with an eraser. Either one works, and both will require a lot of trial, error, and adjustments.

One of the traps when distinguishing values, needs, wants, and behaviors is diminishing the worth of anything outside of core values. In doing so, we start dumping anything that sounds important into the core values category. While they are all important, they are also different from each other. When we intentionally set the flow in the right direction and begin to understand these differences, we are able to realize the full potential all four categories can bring.

While there are not black-and-white distinctions between these four categories, there are important distinguishing nuances to note as you attempt to fill each column. This exercise, to differentiate them, is designed to create an awareness of the systemic relationship among the four columns. This is why an electronic spreadsheet or a piece of paper with a sharp pencil and a big eraser may prove helpful. Think of your worksheet as a jigsaw puzzle—you have to experiment by trying out the pieces in different places. It's all part of the discovery as you keep digging to your core.

You might want to assign a brief description to each of the column headings to help you keep them differentiated in your mind. Consider the following:

- A *behavior* is action-oriented and is put into motion in specific situations. You might think of its application as being very situational in a given moment in time.
- A *want* is a desire for something, someone, or somewhere.
- A *need* is deeply foundational in nature, so much so that it often feels like or is mistaken for a core value. You will often see a very direct connection to a value; if not siblings, they are first cousins!
- A *core value* is a principal state of being. It is the central, innermost, or most essential part of anyone. When consistently applied, it sets a trajectory—a flow—into motion. It is what establishes integrity, because integrity is the fabric of each and every value.

Once established and embraced with personal ownership, each value is like a dye poured into the flowing water of the river. It penetrates everything—every need, every want, and every behavior.

As you differentiate and fine-tune, a couple of additional approaches might prove useful. A management theory called Total Quality Management (TQM) involved a lot of intentional measurements that, no doubt, put a lot of unintentional pressure on personal and organizational core values that had probably rarely been thought about. Yet tucked within TQM was the theory that asking the question *why* five times will lead one to the real problem.

Let's say, for example, that you're trying to determine why something went wrong. You would ask: Why did that happen? With the answer to that question, you would ask: Why did *that* happen? Then with the answer to that second question, you would ask why again . . . and again . . . and then one more time. The theory is that the answer to that fifth why (or why[5]) is the real problem and everything else is just a symptom of that problem. The idea purported that until you fixed the why[5] problem, you would continue to experience all the other symptoms. It's useful to note here that we often work on symptoms with quick-fix behavior modification solutions rather than digging to our core values.

This why[5] approach will help you dig closer to your core. You can take the why[5] concept and apply it to your four columns: *Core Values, Needs, Wants,* and *Behaviors.* In doing so, you will create a systematic flow on your worksheet that makes sense to you.

Take any word on your brainstorm list and ask yourself why

it is really important to you. If there is an answer, you have likely moved one step closer from the behavior side of your puzzle toward the core-value side of the puzzle. Then take that answer and ask why it is so important to you. If there is an answer, again you have likely moved one step closer from the behavior side of your puzzle toward the core-value side. I don't know if you will actually make it through all five whys. But I do know that at some point you will ask why and there will be no answer. It just is. At that point, you are most likely at the level of a very deep need or a core value. This process is simply one way to test out the pieces of your puzzle and distinguish which answers go in which columns—keeping in mind the nuances of each of the four categories.

You will likely find that working with your four-column worksheet is not a one-way, linear process. It is helpful to work at it from all sides, trying it from all directions. For instance, some like to try it from the other direction. Take a word that seems to be speaking to you as a core value and substitute the word "because" for "why." Follow this flow: Respect is *core* because I *need* connection. Connection is a *need* because I *want* to engage. Engage is a *want*, and therefore I will actively listen. Active listening becomes the behavior—a behavior far more valuable when grounded in a core value of respect.

While helpful in navigating the flow of your puzzle, this "because" approach can unintentionally send you drifting if you are not careful, especially if you don't keep it others-focused. In the example above, the focus still remains on others. If it becomes about you, then what you find is that even a slight drift introduces pollutants into the mix that can easily begin to use your values in a manipulative way for personal gain. Checking the nature and purity of your motives helps keep the pollutants out of the flow.

As you keep digging to your core, you will develop an ever-greater understanding of the nuances between each of the categories. This will help you intentionally establish an integrated flow that moves in the right direction. Soon, you will become increasingly conscious that almost any need, want, or behavior that is grounded to your core values is exponentially more valuable. As you continue digging, I would suggest small increments of time for this phase. The ideal increment would be a minimum of thirty minutes per sitting (to be sure you can immerse yourself in your thoughts), and no more than one hour, because focused thinking will wane after that. It would be ideal to engage in these sittings two or three times a week over the next month.

Outside of your scheduled sittings, find other times when you can simply let your mind wonder about and wander through the possible values at your core. Throughout these early months, your mind will continually process ideas in the background. It is helpful to periodically check in and bring them to the foreground. This could be while exercising, taking a shower, going for a run or walk, in prayer or meditation, with a glass of wine or mug of beer, or while flying from one destination to another. The

CHECKING THE NATURE AND PURITY OF YOUR MOTIVES HELPS KEEP THE POLLUTANTS OUT OF THE FLOW.

point here is that you have plenty of opportunity to continuously stir your thinking so that different ideas can surface depending on varying types of days, moods, challenges, and accomplishments. This variety of circumstances is why several periodic sittings with your list will give you fresh perspectives, allowing you to reflect from several different angles. There is no question; this is a process—and a paradox of sorts.

Not too far from my home, there was a neighborhood road that ended in an intersection of a well-traveled street. There was a stop sign that evidently wasn't effective enough to prevent accidents. Beneath that stop sign, the city added an additional sign, formally painted in black letters on a white background that simply read, "Look Again."

Those two words are also the invite, insight, and investigative nature of paradox. It is rare, if ever, that we see truth at first glance. Danger can lurk amongst first impressions. Our vision is tainted by our experience, season, and position in life, along with the 20/20 certainty we have unknowingly created in our perspectives.

This can create quite a dilemma in truly connecting to your core. The "big dig" to your core values requires a lot of shoveling, sifting, and looking at what you find. That, in itself, is tedious work. Yet a first glance at what you find is never enough. Deep into your dig, the search for core values ultimately teaches you to look again—and again, and again. It is a defining nature of the digging experience. It can be both frustrating and exhilarating at the same time.

Just as important as your commitment to digging will be the other valuable realizations you discover along the way.

VALUES BEYOND BELIEF

Recently, a great friend texted me a quote she'd come across. It said: "Your beliefs don't make you a better person, your behavior does!" On the surface it made a lot of sense. A lot of quotes make sense on the surface. However, it immediately stimulated my thinking—in two different directions.

The first direction had to do with the "behavior" part of the quote. There are a lot of leadership phrases that rightfully celebrate the importance of behaviors, such as "walk the talk." Years ago, another phrase caught my attention: Your actions are speaking so loud that I can't hear what you're saying!

Organizations have poured billions of dollars into creating behavioral change. Some would argue the return on investment might be questionable. Investments strictly focused on behavioral change can certainly reap short-term results. Yet, when strategies are solely focused on behavior they rarely meet their full potential.

Change in your behavior may allow others to like you better, but in and of themselves, behaviors do not make you a better person. While your behaviors may win the approval of others, they can be quite deceiving. If behaviors alone made you a better person then the motives behind your behaviors wouldn't really matter. And what's behind your behaviors does matter.

Behaviors matter too. They always will, but they will always be a better lagging indicator rather than a leading indicator of who you are.

CHANGE IN YOUR BEHAVIOR
MAY ALLOW OTHERS TO
LIKE YOU BETTER, BUT IN
AND OF THEMSELVES,
BEHAVIORS DO NOT MAKE YOU
A BETTER PERSON.

My thinking also pulled me back to the "belief" part of the quote. I do believe the first part of the quote is correct: "Your beliefs don't make you a better person." It got me thinking about beliefs vs. core values. It forced me to make a distinction I hadn't fully recognized before: ingrained beliefs are not the same as core values. Our beliefs are often nurtured within our strong opinions.

We seem to know a lot more about behaviors and beliefs than we do core values. It should be no surprise, since we tend to spend a lot more time talking about them. And my experience has been that we would much prefer to focus on behavior and beliefs than do the hard work required of digging to our core.

This is fully understandable. Beliefs and behaviors are like drywall and the paint that covers it. Our values are like the two-by-fours that hold them in place. It's easier to paint the drywall that is hung on decaying two-by-fours than it is to rebuild what's behind it. It will, in fact, look better for some period of time. Yet it's the two-by-fours that hold the potential to make a stronger wall. Similarly, core values hold the potential to make you a better person.

This is not a chicken-or-the-egg kind of proposition. Thinking behaviors is what makes you a better person is more like putting the cart before the horse. Both core values and behaviors are important, but knowing which should impact the other is critical: your values should impact your behaviors and your beliefs.

I am painfully aware how much easier it is to paint the wall than to replace it. Again, I'm by no means diminishing the importance or impact of our behaviors. Once the two-by-fours are constructed, the drywall and paint are really important. Defining our core values without a resulting change in behavior creates a significant investment with no return. Behaviors fueled by intentionally focused core values create a much better scenario—and likely a better person.

Come to think of it, behaviors actually do have something to do with beliefs. They're what eventually make our core values believable to others. Our core values, in turn, make our behaviors sustainable. Over time, they have the potential to not only make us better people but also help others become better people too.

KNEADED BY YOUR NEEDS

I have found paradoxical wisdom in the spirit of this quote that has been shared in various ways throughout the years, and most recently attributed to hip-hop artist Joseph Simmons: "The richest person in the world is not the one who has the most but the one who needs the least." One might conclude that it is, therefore, wise and important to manage your needs. When our needs are not fueled by our core values, we drift in a direction toward addiction. We soon become the dough in the making of the bread; we are kneaded by our needs. Over time, your needs will get a firm grip on your core and knead you and your values all about.

Remember that powerful question that was tucked into the bottom right corner on the cover of a *Fast Company* magazine back in the era of ever-increasing abundance of the late 1990s: When is enough, enough?" It's a timeless question. Defined limits (e.g., determining when enough is enough) are the essence of core values and the paradoxical nature of their endless potential. Left unanswered, it will only be a matter of time until you start to drift and then ultimately become kneaded by your needs.

Yet willpower and self-imposed restrictions only go so far and frankly are not very inspiring or fulfilling. The problem with such a disciplined approach is that the expended energy is aimed as a point of resistance or containment.

We have noted the importance of behaviors, wants, needs, and core values. More importantly, we have noted the importance in which direction the four of them flow. When our flow is moving in the right direction, our energy is spent engaging our needs rather than resisting them. The richest may not only be the one who needs the least; the richest may also be the one who realizes it. The richness of our needs is much more about the source than the quantity.

WHEN OUR FLOW IS MOVING IN THE RIGHT DIRECTION, OUR ENERGY IS SPENT ENGAGING OUR NEEDS RATHER THAN RESISTING THEM.

SUBTLETIES MATTER

As you start digging for your core values, it's really important to start with the right question. That simple question is: What *are my* values?

When you replace "are my" with "do I" you get a completely different question. While it forces you to change the last word from plural form to singular, it also changes it from a noun into a verb—more importantly into a desire. It's amazing how two different words in the midst of a question can completely change where you start digging. And more importantly, change what you will find.

The question "what do I value?" isn't a bad question. In fact, it can be helpful to flesh out some very important wants and needs. Starting there, however, can be misguiding. In fact, you may very well come to "value" something that is in contradiction to a core value. That is much more likely when you start exploring what you value without digging for what your values are.

Subtleties matter, as do the specifics you discover at your core when you start with the right question.

AN EQUATION EXAMINATION

Definitions often limit our thinking, while metaphors tend to expand it. Metaphors help us understand what something is like. They make for wonderful and welcoming signposts along any journey—or on any dig. Recently, I blindly ran into one of those signposts. This insight sat within the mathematics of adding, subtracting, multiplying, and dividing.

While needs, wants, and behaviors have elements of all four mathematical characteristics, core values only embrace three of them. Core values can add depth, insight, and understanding. They can bring focus and clarity by subtracting what is unnecessary, unhealthy, and undermining. And core values can inform and multiply the quality of our needs, wants, and behaviors to an exponential level. As I stood gazing at this metaphoric signpost, one thing seemed to gain clarity for me: *Core values do not divide.*

Most any behavior, want, or need can hold a divisible characteristic. Core values don't. They eliminate division rather than create it.

I invite you over to this signpost to ponder for a while. Maybe the mathematical elements of this equation are more than a signpost. They may very well be a metaphoric microscope under which you can analyze the sometimes-subtle differences among behaviors, wants, needs, and core values.

It's worth a look inside.

THE INTERRELATED NATURE OF CORE VALUES

While we may come to the insight of our core values one at a time, they will ultimately become a package deal. They work in unison with one another. While core values bring strength to your needs, wants, and behaviors, they bring the most strength to each other when they are integrated. Therein lies the birth of your integrity. This means your core values influence one another at their source.

It is helpful to consciously think about how each of your core values influences all the other core values on your list. You will find opportunities to bring further depth to your values by doing this. It is this intentional integration that makes your core uniquely you!

At the same time, you will find contradictions. At least, that is how they appear on the surface. And if not contradictions, you will feel like one value may compete with another. And it will certainly feel that way in certain situations as you are trying to live them.

For the sake of clarity, I like to think of them as combined resources. In any given situation, one value may need to take the lead, while never being disconnected from any of the others. Any value taking the lead is still accountable to all the other values with which it is integrated. It's important that your own core values remain integrated too.

But that doesn't mean that in any given situation they are in perfect balance. I remember a conversation years ago with

IT'S IMPORTANT THAT YOUR OWN CORE VALUES REMAIN INTEGRATED TOO.

my friend Kevin. We were talking about the big trend at that time, which was to create balance in your life. Kevin's perspective always stuck with me. He said, "I believe this balance thing is a figment of our imagination. Life is more like a pendulum that swings back and forth. It isn't about balance; it's about keeping your eye on the pendulum and asking if it is where it should be at the time."

I didn't realize it then, but doing as he said would be hard, if not impossible, if you weren't clear on your own core values. I would say the strength of your core values is the best diagnostic tool of your pendulum. Sometimes one value takes the lead while still remaining accountable to all the others. It's the only way they remain integrated—it's precisely why integrity is not a core value. Rather, it is the fabric of every value.

The integration of your core values doesn't happen automatically. It must happen intentionally, every day. Our values have to be activated on a regular basis. Otherwise, the flow gets messed up again, and instead of our core values doing the driving, the burden shifts to our needs, wants, and behaviors. And just like the non-core parts of our body, our needs, wants, and behaviors will try—and succeed—to pick up a load they were never designed to carry, and there will be a heavy price to pay later.

THE BLEND OF SCIENCE AND SPIRITUAL

Another common question I'm asked is, "Where do core values come from?" It's a great question, yet one that could completely misguide you. It's worth pondering—as well as all the other questions that you are likely to unearth in your deep dig—yet it is also one that could encourage you to lay down your shovel and simply embrace something you have experienced before. In other words, to run to what is comfortable—in many cases your ingrained wants, needs, opinions, and beliefs.

As you dig your well, foot after foot, you will initially have a plethora of data points to sort through. Some of those data points will come from your own life experiences: family, friends, education, decisions, successes, failures, and transitions. It can be quite helpful to create a lifeline and revisit some of these key points, lessons learned, and how, individually and collectively, they may have shaped you—for better or for worse. As you continue to dig, you will become increasingly aware of perhaps which is which. Other data points can come from meaningful conversations you currently experience with those who mean the most to you, those who embrace you, and, yes, those who seem to see many things completely different than you.

You may have access to your results from a number of well-researched instruments you have taken in the workplace as part of a workshop or professional development program. In fact, by now, you may feel a bit like a lab rat with the endless number of self-assessment instruments available today to assess any aspect of your existence. Many of them can be insightful data points if you let them inform you. While they can be especially revealing when it comes to your behaviors, wants, and needs, you should never let them define your core values. Your core is for you to discover as you continue to dig past these data points. In the meantime, the data from each one of them and the insights you gain from your systemic glance at the collective message across all of them can bring a scientific foundation for your early stages of digging. They will be very helpful for as far as they go.

Then you will need to rest your scientific shovel for a while. While much of this data will bring useful thoughts, some of it will bring distractions. Noticing both will be revealing as you move from a scientific phase to a much more spiritually reflective phase. It seems that we often put the scientific and the spiritual into isolated silos. Like core values, they are not separate; they are systemic. It will enhance your digging if you allow them to enrich each other throughout. It is likely you will find it helpful to move back and forth between these two phases for some period of time.

Ultimately, the deeper you dig your well, the more you will find it useful to move increasingly toward a more contemplative stage of your discovery. But let's not get ahead of ourselves. A lot of interesting scientific digging awaits. I hope you have at it and fill your mind. I also hope you will put down your shovel and pause every now and then to stir your heart and soul by periodically digesting the remainder of this Discovery section.

Rather than setting a direction, each of the remaining segments of this Discovery section is simply designed to stir your thinking and invite you to go beyond.

Pause Point

- As you look back on how you thought about your core values, which of your values might have been behaviors, wants, or needs—especially those you would consider to be wonderful, deeply seated behaviors, wants, and needs?

- How are the nuances between behaviors, wants, needs, and values bringing further clarification and/or confusion?

- At this point in your dig, your discovery, where are you feeling resistance/openness?

QUESTIONING THE UNQUESTIONABLE

Digging is more likely to raise questions than to provide answers. Yet a desire for efficiency can often create a seductively quick jump to all-too-familiar solutions. This seems to be where we often want to put our energy. It can make us feel smarter and certainly gives us a chance to stir the pot of our wants, needs, opinions, and beliefs—all with great intention.

Recently, I was speaking with a group of business professionals. At this event, it is protocol for the speaker to come with four or five relevant questions to be used for table discussion. But I decided to try a new approach. I presented for about forty minutes. When it came time for table discussion, I told the group that rather than bringing my questions, I wanted to invite them to use the time to discern the questions my presentation brought to mind for them. I first asked them to sit quietly and individually think of their own questions.

I then asked them to share their questions with each other without discussing reactions, thoughts, or answers—just question upon question upon question. My hope was that one question might invite another question.

What do you think I heard when the exchange began? At most tables, the exchange almost immediately turned to discussion without question. It reminded me how our tendency is to jump to solutions, opinions, and reactions rather than deepen our wonder by leaping from the curiosity sparked by questions.

As you dig, the questions you unearth don't need to be

DIGGING IS MORE LIKELY
TO RAISE QUESTIONS
THAN TO PROVIDE ANSWERS.

immediately answered. More likely their inquiry needs to marinate within you a bit. Rather than feel the need to answer your every question, let each question stimulate the next one.

My good friend, Master Certified Coach Mary Jo Hazard, has taught me a great deal about the art and value of great questions. When it comes to core values, these are a few she brings to mind. They may trigger some insightful answers for you, but my greater hope is that they stir even more inspiring questions within you.

- How does it serve you, your organization, and our world to name and fully live your core values?

- How does it cost you and our world if you don't name and fully live your values?

- When something really annoys, frustrates, and upsets you, what's the connection with that and your core values?

- Alternatively, when something brings you great joy and meaning, how does that connect with your core values?

- How do your core values help you build relationships with others?

- How do your core values tie in to the legacy you're leaving in your family, your organization, and our world?

I encourage you to spend a few minutes with each of these questions, noting what each of them call forth from within you— and, most importantly, what additional questions do they surface?

A SIGHT UNSEEN

A decade ago, following the surprising experience of suffering my first detached retina, I would often recall that experience by saying, "When you must keep your eyes closed for several days in a row, it's amazing what you'll see!" It was, and is, a paradoxical truth. I would rediscover that truth again in 2010, awaiting the recovery of a retinal detachment in my other eye.

Then six years later, I would revisit that paradoxical truth for a third time. You might say this third retinal detachment blind-sided me! It was all too familiar in some ways, yet it was a completely new experience. Nothing repeated is ever precisely the same.

This is true in a job, a relationship, an adventure, a challenge, or a task of any kind. While the nature of the repeated experience may be the same, we are not. We are different. And, therefore, anything repeated becomes a new experience and creates new opportunities if we choose to creatively embrace them.

My third verse of the same song held a familiar tune of required limitations. The timing, however, presented the challenge of meeting new commitments previously made. My limitations prohibited both air travel and driving, but long-distance train travel remained an option. It was the cumulative seventy hours on the rails that made me question just how viable an option it might prove to be.

The next thing I knew, I was seated at Chicago's Union Station late on a Saturday night, awaiting my 9:30 p.m. departure

NOTHING REPEATED

IS EVER PRECISELY THE SAME.

for the East Coast. Just three weeks post-surgery, the nine-day excursion seemed a bit overwhelming. As I sat in my passenger window seat, there was only one thing I needed to do: look out the window.

Windows on airplanes offer their own fascinating views, but they are very different than the windows on a train. While smaller, airplane windows ironically provide the portal to a big picture: broad strokes, you might say. While you see a lot through them, you miss almost everything that is right before your eyes. You miss what is there. The threads that create the fabric of your vast scenic experience are real but not visible. But just because we can't see them doesn't make them less valid, less real, or less important. It just means we are, in effect, blinded from what they may hold to teach us, remind us, or give us.

The windows on trains are large and revealing. They pass places that even cars on a freeway never pass. They hold a kinship to the car windows that historically traveled two-lane highways through the heart of little towns. They travel through the authentic realness of everyday life and all it honestly reveals. These windows don't have the opportunity to protect you from anything that comes before them. They offer no well-spun, catchy brands or taglines as polished veneers.

They provide equal opportunity in presenting the good, the bad, and the ugly without discriminating or judging the value each of them hold. In doing so, these windows reveal truth, along with the unique beauty that only truth has the right to hold.

They weave the threads of walls of graffiti with the harvested fields of farms. Factories and homes, large and small, new and old, are blended into a mosaic of one continuous picture. And within each scene is a unique story to be told. These windows-of-the-rails allow your mind to wander and your heart to wonder if you let them. And if you look through these windows long enough, they become mirrors into your soul.

These mirrors reveal truth. Or at least the invitation to seek it. It's an invitation that is hard to see and harder to seek in a world seduced with broader strokes.

The broad strokes can be enticing and misguiding. In fact, they can cause you to miss many things. They can eventually cause you to miss what is most important and ultimately most everything that is true. The various stories along the rails are just as connected as the rails themselves. Bolted together, no, but none-theless connected. Our blindness to their blendedness doesn't change them. It simply changes us, and in the process unplugs our sense of connection and appreciation. Truth becomes a sight unseen. The same can happen to our core.

BEYOND THE COMFORTER

Who doesn't want to stay under a cozy comforter just a few more moments on a cold winter morning? The name of this cover-up is so fitting—*so comforting*. Snug and tucked-in seems so perfect. And it is perfect, up to a point. And then, it no longer serves us very well. Eventually, never pulling ourselves out from under the cover would have a devastating impact. The same can hold true for the comfortable behaviors, wants, needs, opinions, and beliefs we snuggle up to along the course of our life.

Twenty-two years ago, when I first launched my career in professional speaking, I set out on a quest to uncover some unique stories of exponential leaps of development. I repeatedly inquired: Describe a time when you experienced a period of exponential personal growth.

The stories varied widely, but they all had one theme in common. Each had to do with a time of significant transition: sudden change, tragic loss, failure, or a moment of unexpected truth. At the same time, there was one theme that never showed up in any of the responses: a season of success.

Yet success is what we desire, strategize for, strive for, and in some cases, die for. And there is no question that success can deliver its own teachable moments. Unfortunately, it doesn't seem to provide the context for periods of exponential personal growth. At least it hadn't for even one single person whom I asked. That is, until that success ended or was taken away.

I'm certainly not suggesting that the lesson here is to avoid success. I am suggesting, however, that success has its limits. In many ways, our own success can not only provide the comforts of life but it can also become the comforter of our life. And under the comforter of life we can become seduced and eventually addicted to the comfort. It is precisely why entitlement knows no one specific demographic.

I'm also not suggesting that we go looking for tragic loss or failure. But I am suggesting that we might want to get up and go looking for the uncomfortable, the uncertain, the unfamiliar, and the unknown.

We can learn and grow in the midst of most any circumstance. It just seems that we are more willing, open, and vulnerable in times of transition. Transition has a way of tilling the soil of our soul.

And so does the uncomfortable. Maybe you have sensed this in a conversation with someone experiencing an uncomfortable season. Compare that to a conversation with somebody in the midst of success. Most often, while the latter may be more fun, the former is likely to prove more meaningful.

We could all benefit by pulling ourselves out from under the comforter: communicating more with those who don't think like us, embracing those who don't look like us, and, yes, hanging with those who make us a little—or a lot—uncomfortable. It makes digging to your core much more valuable.

After all, we might eventually discover just how comfortable being uncomfortable can be, and in doing so, we might experience a season of exponential personal growth and perhaps even reveal another core value.

UNDER THE COMFORTER
OF LIFE WE CAN BECOME
SEDUCED AND EVENTUALLY
ADDICTED TO THE COMFORT.

LOOK FOR NOW

I am often asked, "Are the words I'm looking for to describe my core values simply descriptions of my recent behaviors and choices, or are they descriptions of my aspirations?" The answer is neither. While it's a fair question, neither the past nor the future are that helpful in your process of discovery.

Many leadership books suggest that if you want to know someone's core values, all you have to do is look at their checkbook or calendar; it's there that you'll see how they spend their money and their time. I've certainly fallen for this, and I've even suggested it to others. It makes for a nice cliché, but it is a judgmental and damning proposition for others and ourselves.

We have no idea if someone's checkbook or calendar reflects the values at their core. We don't even know if our own checkbook and calendar reflect the values at our core. This is especially true if we have never taken a journey to our core. The reason has to do specifically with a concept we noted before: *the drift*.

Rather than look to the past or the future, it's far more helpful to stay in the present and dig for the truth. You won't find that truth in your behaviors, wants, or needs, nor will you find it in your checkbook or calendar. You will find it through your patience and persistence to keep digging to your core. Once you find that truth, I have no doubt you will find the inspiration to move your current conditions (checkbook, calendar, behaviors, wants, needs, and all) toward the truth of those values at your core.

RATHER THAN LOOK TO
THE PAST OR THE FUTURE,
IT'S FAR MORE HELPFUL
TO STAY IN THE PRESENT
AND DIG FOR THE TRUTH.

You won't find the truth overnight. Nor will you align your behaviors, wants, and needs overnight. The core values you discover will help you align them over time.

Your digging will prove aspirational enough.

THE REALITY OF TRUTH

I was sitting out by the fireless fire pit in the Las Vegas backyard of my great friend Shawn Williams. We were having one of those conversations that matter—you know, beyond the surface level of sports and weather. Our talk was genuine, meaningful, and vulnerable, sharing back and forth. Then wisdom stumbled out of Shawn's mouth: "It's real, but it's just not true." It immediately caught my attention. It was an insight that deserved its own conversation.

Fearful that Shawn would say it first, I quickly replied: "Hmm. Real vs. true. You ought to write a book on that!" As anticipated, he shot back with: "I was just getting ready to tell *you* that!" Maybe it will deserve a book someday, even knowing the likelihood that a plethora have already been penned about it.

Nonetheless, in subsequent conversations, Shawn and I have noticed numerous examples of the gaps between what is real and what is true. The implications are wide and varied.

It feels, today, that we are experiencing more than just a drought of truth. It seems we may be experiencing an increasing lack of desire for the truth. So much has jumped in front of truth: labels, bias, prejudice, cliques, tribes, boundaries, expediency, convenience, and self- and group-justification. Fattened up on spin and sensationalism, we are starving for truth.

Anchored in foxholes, we can fall into the trap of listening to what confirms our reality rather than challenging it. It's completely understandable. It feels better to embrace a sense of quick confirmation. We can feel smarter and justified. Oh yes, and then there is that sense of being correct. It's as good as a warm blanket wrapping our own ego in comfort. And the experience of it all is very real. Believe me, I have used plenty of those blankets myself.

It is often said that perception is reality. How true that is. Yet reality is not always truth. Frequently, reality is not truth at all. I fully understand that I'm climbing out on a weak limb here, because in a quick search in Dictionary.com or Webster.com you will see that each, in part, uses "reality" in the very definition of truth. I would concede that some reality is truth, but not all truth is the reality we create.

And without a genuine desire for truth beyond all else, we are far more likely to deepen the reality we experience—whether it's truth or not. Rarely do we do this intentionally, which is what makes it all the more dangerous.

It is precisely why being blind to the truth at our core, while pouring endless time, effort, energy, and emotion into our needs, wants, and behaviors is a formula for a false reality. This is precisely why getting to the truth is worth the dig.

WITHOUT A GENUINE DESIRE
FOR TRUTH BEYOND ALL ELSE,
WE ARE FAR MORE LIKELY
TO DEEPEN THE REALITY
WE EXPERIENCE—
WHETHER IT'S TRUTH OR NOT.

LET IT GO, LET IT GO, LET IT GO!

In preparation for my last presentation of the calendar year, I felt as if I had chosen the wrong topic at the wrong time. I had been with the audience I would be presenting to about fifteen months prior, when I had presented on a topic that had felt right: love is all you need. That topic seemed to resonate with this thriving, interfaith group at Monarch Landing, a wonderful retirement community on the north side of my hometown of Naperville, Illinois. In fact, in the year that followed, they set a theme for all their speakers: love-in-action.

I was the caboose of that year-long run of speakers who had volunteered to visit this wonderful group throughout the year. That's a lot of "love" to hear about. And it seemed, just hours before Christmas, that a syrupy encore to my "Love Is All You Need" presentation was in order.

But something inside kept drawing me to a completely different idea. I felt compelled to do a presentation on letting go. That topic morphed into the love of letting go. Since this idea wouldn't let go of me, I decided to go with it.

I knew walking in that the audience had already let go of so many things. And right from the beginning, I confessed, with the packed house in front of me, my complete reservation about my chosen topic. I acknowledged their expertise and told them that I could spend an entire afternoon sitting with each of them learning far more about letting go of things than I could ever share with them.

I then recounted my experience, as a five-year-old, of acciden-
tally letting go of my white helium balloon and how doing so
had created a well-grounded disdain for letting go of anything.
Maybe to prove my point, I brought a massive white helium balloon with me to the presentation. The balloon perched on a long
white ribbon. The ribbon allowed the balloon to reach to the
very top of the huge Christmas tree to my right, yet grounded
the balloon's freedom and the innate potential it had to fly.

I then talked about how not everything we need to let go of
is on the outside. In fact, the most challenging and most important things are on the inside. I decided to slowly and reflectively
share a few examples for clarification. For some it might be an
unfulfilled dream, when life hadn't turned out precisely as we had
so strategically planned. It could be a regret or disappointment
in ourselves or someone else. For others, it could be a long-held
grudge, and for others, it could be a belief in which we have sunk
our teeth so deeply that we repel others in the way we claim it.
Then there are those expectations that we create for something or
from someone. For others, there is a tight embrace of traditions
deeply seeded. For some, it's an untold secret. And for many it is
fear itself. For most, it's possibly a systemic connection of a few
of these.

I suggested that the love of letting go was a perfect theme for
the Christmas season. For all of us, there is always another package to unwrap, inside of us, precisely so we can let it go. And in

doing so, we become more loving, more loveable, and more like the story that Christmas brings.

I then returned to the white helium balloon. I offered up the possibility that holding on creates a deceptively fulfilling experience and in doing so keeps us from the opportunity of experiencing the wonder of true flight. I then meant to suggest that as we entered the New Year, that whenever we encounter a helium balloon, we could let it gently nudge us with encouragement to open yet one more package inside of us and let it go. But caught up in the closing moment of my presentation, I totally forgot to mention it.

It was the whole purpose and lasting intent of my white helium balloon metaphor. As I drove home, I became aware of my omission and became increasingly bummed about it. As I pulled into my driveway waiting for the garage door to ascend, I had to laugh at the irony and just let it go!

As you dig for your core values, you will inevitably become increasingly aware of some behaviors, wants, needs, beliefs, and opinions you should let go.

GRAVITATIONAL PULL

Growing up, I was always fascinated by the adventures of our space program. NASA's space shuttle program was particularly intriguing to me. The graceful return landings were incredible to watch. They were quite an advancement from capsules splashing into the ocean. The smooth landings were also quite the contrast to the thrust of energy required from the very beginning of the mission.

I have often referenced shuttle lift-offs for comparison's sake to any significant new beginning. I would propose that the greatest energy expenditure of the shuttle launch was in the first half-inch of lift-off. I don't know if I'm scientifically correct, but I think you get the point. Getting started often requires a significant energy expenditure, including an engagement of focus and commitment. Ironically, getting started isn't likely the greatest point of resistance when it comes to digging for your core values.

Yes, getting started takes energy, focus, and commitment, but getting started—the lift-off—is manageable compared to what you experience the deeper you dig. I have now heard these words over and over: "Wow, this is really hard!" These telling words don't surface at the beginning of the digging experience. They surface well into the process.

Once the shuttle is in motion it gains momentum, increasing exponentially in speed as it climbs. Beginning the brainstorming of your core values from a blank sheet of paper is much like the energy required at lift-off. Yet, with lift-off, a multitude of ideas often begin to surface at an ever-increasing momentum. Then, in the midst of the beauty of flight, the shuttle meets its greatest resistance: pulling away from the gravitational pull of earth's atmosphere.

This particular segment of flight establishes a necessary breakthrough. It is precisely what stands between all the effort up to that point and a complete lack of resistance on the other side. And it is no minor barrier. Ironically, the point of greatest resistance is also the threshold to a complete breakthrough.

At some point in defining core values, you will meet the gravitational pull. While you'll likely experience some turbulent storms en route, there is nothing like the experience awaiting you the moment you face your gravitational pull. You will meet this gravitational pull individually in defining your own personal core values and then collectively in understanding the intersection of your values and the core values of the organization where you work. Your personal breakthrough may very well be the only thing that equips you to face the magnitude of the gravitational pull you will encounter day-to-day.

Astronauts and the incredible team behind them clearly anticipate the reality and navigational requirements necessary to pierce the resistance awaiting. It comes as no surprise, nor is it ever easy. It is simply necessary.

As I was in the midst of writing the manuscript for *Return On Integrity*, it seemed the gravitational pull within the writing process was endless. An increasing lack of clarity in how to express

AT SOME POINT IN DEFINING
CORE VALUES, YOU WILL MEET
THE GRAVITATIONAL PULL.

on the page what seemed to be clear in my head was a gravitational pull that added new meaning to writer's block.

I was determined to push my way through the resistance. It was once again a cold, dreary winter day in Chicagoland. I'd arrived early at the Morton Arboretum for a morning of planning this "push" for action. My friends Al and Mary Jo were meeting me there for lunch. I was quite proud of my push plan and was looking forward to getting their feedback. As always, they were angels of encouragement. But what really changed everything was when Al said, "I think your missing piece is just saying *yes*." I comprehended just enough of what he meant "to just keep 'showing-up' with my *yes*" to understand that *yes* would keep me moving deeper. It did, and it still does.

Coming to *yes* in the midst of what seems to be resistance allows you to embrace what *is*—whatever it is—as you continue to dig for the clarity of the core values within you. Knowing that you have persevered through a prior resistance can be of limited assurance as it only represents what was. But your renewed *yes* allows you to keep digging into what is.

Gravitational pull is a gift. And your *yes* is what you use to open it. It makes the shovel just a little lighter each time you say *yes* to picking it up again and digging just a little more deeply. As difficult as it may be, anticipating what's on the other side will always make it worthwhile.

THE POISE IN A PAUSE

In a society that values ever-increasing speeds, vast volumes, and packing more into every passing moment, waiting is often seen as wasted time. Even worthless. Activity is held in high regard. Movement is seen as synonymous with momentum. Organizations feel pressure to bring a product to market first. The media feel the pressure of being the first to break a story. Our need for speed may be breaking all of us.

In such a society, individuals are likely to feel the self-imposed guilt from a period of inactivity. They may experience the judgmental inference of the busy people around them. Busy is often worn as a badge of honor. Just ask someone how they are doing. Odds are, their short answer will be the word (or contain the word) "busy." It's most likely an accurate response. In fact, they'll likely front-end the word "busy" with a descriptive modifier like "really," "incredibly," or "super" to ensure you know just how busy they are, because just being "busy" isn't quite good enough anymore.

The word "busy" makes for a strange answer to someone asking how you are doing. In most cases, the answer isn't really an answer. It's more a reflex. Reflexes become more unconsciously common when we're really, or incredibly, or super busy. At the same time, while "busy" may very well impact how you are doing, it doesn't actually answer the question. It defines a level of activity but not your actual state of being. Sometimes it is a subconscious coverup for it.

This sense of "busy" mixed with a dash of "hurry" will lead your digging to a plethora of more behaviors, wants, and needs, some of which may be very good ones. But they won't be core values. The busyness will likely be accompanied by a fading sense of integrity and a higher risk of drifting.

Our moment in time in this world offers increasing options for busy. Just in the last twenty years, the exponential increase of opportunities to make yourself busy is breathtaking. Anyone who wants to be busy, can be. Yet just because you can be doesn't mean you should be. A lot has been lost in business—and more importantly, life—amongst all the busy-ness.

Somewhere in our mix of buying busy as better, we have wasted away the worth in waiting.

I'm not talking about passive waiting where lazy hides itself in disguise. Nor am I talking about just waiting around for someone else to take on a responsibility that is yours. Passive waiting cultivates anxiety.

I'm talking about *active* waiting. Sometimes we're simply supposed to wait, and the worth of the wait comes when we choose to embrace our waiting. It's hard to fully embrace anything when you're on the run. Waiting is an opportunity that actually invites our embrace. Active waiting nurtures anticipation.

It's not that we haven't experienced the worth of waiting. I'm sure, in the end, most of us have expressed the sentiment, "It was worth waiting for!" It's not so hard to see the worth in retrospect. It's far more valuable to see the worth in the midst of the wait,

ACTIVE WAITING

NURTURES ANTICIPATION.

knowing something is worth waiting for. Active waiting is a great teacher. It teaches us about patience, gratitude, and the real value of what we ultimately experience. Active waiting is not an excuse. It's a strategy.

Embracing waiting takes practice, so let's get practical. You can begin by embracing the next red traffic light you encounter. Red lights are a great example of the worth in waiting. Ignore the wait of a red light and you're likely to be blindsided while also blindsiding someone else. Red lights can serve as a built-in accountability partner every time you encounter one. Let each red light ask you how you're doing at waiting! Let these lights encourage you to tighten your embrace around that for which you're actively awaiting.

Active waiting is a pause with poise. It's the moment between what is and what will be. It's only temporary if what we hope to be is meant to be. The poise in our pause unleashes the freedom to find peace in our waiting. It's in the poise that we begin to understand that active waiting is filled with momentum. All that happens in active waiting, often unseen, is a bit of a paradox. It outpaces the accomplishments of busyness at almost every turn.

In digging for your core values, you will find that there is a fair amount of waiting between the time you first pick up your shovel and the moment your core values are vaguely clear enough to embrace. Active waiting is not idle. And sometimes it happens in complete silence.

FORCED FIELD ANALYSIS

In my very younger years, I loved the rides of amusement parks. I especially loved the ones that would spin and mess with your equilibrium. Two of my favorites were the Twister and the Scrambler.

Another amusement ride I found fascinating was simple in design but held an important lesson within. Everyone entered a large round room and stood with their back to the wall, facing the center. The room started spinning and gradually picked up speed. As the spinning cylinder reached top speeds, the floor slowly began dropping and didn't stop until it was eight feet lower than it had been at the start of the ride. No one inside the spinning cylinder dropped with the floor. The force held them firmly in place with their back against the wall. The reason was obvious, but it was also invisible. A force field was at play, and force fields can be tough to break through.

It's become increasingly clear to me that the struggle for an individual to see, feel, and eventually understand their core is not a cognitive issue. No matter how many clarifying questions get answered regarding the nature of core values, there will likely be more questions, frustration, and confusion. That is, until an invisible force field is penetrated.

It's the force field I encountered at a secluded writers' venue in Virginia while I was writing *Return On Integrity*. The force field was indeed invisible. I couldn't touch it or hug it, but I could certainly feel it. And while I couldn't hear it, in so many ways it was so loud that it was impossible to ignore. And it wasn't that I hadn't experienced it before. In fact, we all experience drops of it at some point every day, but we don't usually experience it to the depth or length I experienced it in Virginia. It was the force field I had to penetrate to experience a breakthrough in my writing. I am convinced we have to experience it on the way to our core. It was uncomfortable and at times almost unbearable. It's *silence*.

I should have known better. I have watched a group of successful healthcare executives unable to endure even a ten-minute prescription of it. I'm not talking about an hour of silence followed by a discussion with others about the experience. In the case of these healthcare executives, some only made it ninety seconds after being instructed to sit in complete silence and ponder a provided question for just ten minutes. Most ended their silence with the majority of the minutes remaining. The problem is that you can never penetrate what you end prematurely.

At my writer's retreat, I endured days of complete silence with no one around to debrief about it and no reasonable way to end it. I suppose I could have run from it—which I actually considered for a moment—but I couldn't end it. Unlike penetrating the force field of the spinning cylinder of my amusement ride, you can't muster a force of energy to push through silence. Silence is something unto which you surrender. In the midst of your consent to silence, you begin to hear and see with increasing clarity the invisible, the essence of what resides within your core.

SILENCE IS SOMETHING
UNTO WHICH YOU SURRENDER.

While this notion of silence may sound simple, it was a huge revelation to me as to why it's been so difficult for smart, successful professionals to make an authentic connection to their core. A mile-long list of answered questions will never add up to the clarity that days of deafening silence will reveal.

I suppose, in years gone by, that there were wonderful sessions of silence naturally experienced on many a front porch. In our world today, that silence is far less likely unless we create it—and then surrender to it. When we choose to embrace the value of silence, that silence will take us to the values at our core.

ONCE UPON A STARRY NIGHT

The same night sky looks very different when viewed through the glow of a major city than it does from the darkness of a tucked-away mountain settlement. Yet the millions of stars are there whether you see them on not; their existence doesn't depend on you seeing them.

Recently, while staying in the Ozarks of southern Missouri, I was reminded of what I'm missing from my common city view of the night sky. It took the magnificence of an Ozark night sky to remind me of the magnitude of that difference. I didn't only see the difference, I felt it.

The glow and glare of city life can blind you to the reality of the sky above you. More importantly, multiple, less impressive distractions often prevent you from looking up.

I remember as a child, stretching out on the green summer grass in my own backyard, looking up at starry nights. I would take in the vast plethora of stars as my vision searched for focus. A familiar poem would come to mind: Star-light star-bright, first star I see tonight. I wish I may, I wish I might have this wish I wish tonight.

I'm sure the many wishes I cast upon those starry summer nights were always about some desire for the future. They were grounded in a perceived need for tomorrow or a wanted dream for months and possibly years ahead. And not to be wishy-washy, I'm sure I cast each wish with a sense of strategic pursuit.

Yet as I look back, I can't recall a single one of those wishes. They seemed so important at the time. I'm sure every cast wish felt just as isolated and focused as the vision of my eyes upon a single star. No doubt, each wish fueled a sense of hope beyond the ground upon which I stretched. I'm certain each wish was informed and influenced by my past. Yet every wish missed one thing: the present.

While I have no doubt that I noticed the vast starry night, I wished for something else. I never realized the wish was already upon me—above me, beside me, within me.

Digging to your core is like stretching out under a starry summer night without the wishing. The wish is already present. The stars are already there. It is about noticing the magnificence above you, beside you, and within you.

Ultimately, digging for your values isn't about finding them. It's about being present so each one of them can find you. Just as I used to search the vast night sky to find that one star to wish upon, I'm certain the one star I noticed had first found me.

Digging is not about the past or the future. It is about being present so you can be found by your core values. Once found, you will notice that there is only one place your core values can be lived—in the present.

ULTIMATELY, DIGGING FOR YOUR VALUES ISN'T ABOUT FINDING THEM. IT'S ABOUT BEING PRESENT SO EACH ONE OF THEM CAN FIND YOU.

THE VALUE OF YOUR MEMORY

For the last twenty-two years, I have had the opportunity to speak with students at the University of Wisconsin—Madison as they begin their major in accounting. This past year, one student asked a question that I have received so many times from professionals well into their careers: "How many core values should you have?" It's a logical question that I don't believe has a numerical answer.

I responded as I always do: "I don't know, but I'm certain of this: It's really hard to live what you can't remember!" Your memory bank is the first test in assessing the value of a list of personal core values. The same is true for organizational core values. Unfortunately, it's a test the owners, leaders, and employees of most organizations fail. You first have to intellectualize your values on the pathway to internalizing them.

Beyond quantity, another frequent inquisition is about proximity: "How do you know when you've arrived?"

The first time it was asked, I reflexively asked, "Arrived where?" The participant responded, "Arrived at your core." Again, it was a logical question, especially in our goal-oriented, finish-line-focused mentality. In other words, "When can I stop looking and start living?"

After a pause to consider her question, I suggested that there is nowhere to arrive. I have come to realize that in your persistent search for your core values, you actually won't find them.

I know that doesn't sound encouraging. The encouraging part is *they find you!*

Your values don't just show up. As you continue to dig, they ever-so-slowly begin to reveal themselves, one at a time. That feeling of "having arrived" becomes irrelevant. Packaged in its own revelation comes an invitation to move from intellectualizing to internalizing, and ultimately from internalizing to living that core value.

That possibility for revelation begins the moment you pick up your shovel.

IT'S REALLY HARD TO LIVE
WHAT YOU CAN'T REMEMBER!

Pause Point

- As you continue to dig and discover, where are you feeling most comfortable and possibly most uncomfortable?

- How often have you experienced silence—complete silence for more than a moment or two? How much can you relate to the earlier example of the healthcare executives who struggled to be in silence for more than a handful of seconds when challenged to ten minutes?

- To better understand your experience with silence, sit in ten minutes of complete silence once a day for the next seven days. Intentionally pick different times of the day to note the differences. After each sit in silence note what the experience was like for you. What was most challenging? What was most surprising? How is the experience changing or not changing from day to day?

PERSONAL VALUES ARE PERSONAL, RIGHT?

At some point, the professional side of us is bound to kick in and question what all this personal stuff has to do with organizations and our work. In fact, after covering so much ground on the very personal front with rarely a mention of the workplace, I'm sure some professionals have cast this experience aside by now. With all the organizational pressures bearing down on the workforce in today's world, who would blame them? There's a part of me that fully understands how this very natural temptation would be so easy to succumb to. Seriously, it all seems—so personal.

Therefore, it's not surprising that people ask: Aren't personal values personal? As in, private? The answer is yes and no. They are very personal and at the same time very systemic in any organization. If you want to understand how non-personal personal values can be, just ask someone who has been part of an organization where there has been a breakdown at the core. The majority will tell you that the personal values of a few systemically impacted everyone. That, in and of itself, becomes very personal for everyone impacted.

Personal core values are never left at the entrance of any organization, however hard you may wish to ignore them. Not only are they not left at the door, they also hold enormous potential for making organizational values exponentially more valuable.

Organizational core values alone are never enough. Even organizations with long-established organizational values have failed to understand the risk in ignoring the powerful impact

ORGANIZATIONAL
CORE VALUES ALONE
ARE NEVER ENOUGH.

of personal values. No matter how much an organization tries to establish healthy organizational core values, if personal core values are ignored, there will always be the risk of an unhealthy undertow shifting the flow of everything. None of this will be intentional, but all of it will be real—and *true*.

Over time, the undertow will begin to strengthen on its own, and before long organizational values will lose strength and eventually become irrelevant. The personal nature of core values is precisely what makes their systemic organizational nature either completely lethal or packed full of enormous potential.

If you were to take only one idea away from this book, I hope it would be this: *The reason most organizational core values have provided limited value is because the personal part of the equation has been ignored or cast aside as not relevant.*

The bottom-line truth when it comes to core values is that there's really no such thing as an organization—period. An organization is, ultimately, nothing more than a collection of people. That gets very personal, whether we like it or not. There's no question, over time, that an organization takes on a personality we call culture, but let's be clear—it remains a collection of people.

Does this mean that organizational values are meaningless? Not at all. They are the fuel for defining the organization's culture. They are a call to who we are collectively—together. It speaks volumes to the whole being greater than the individual parts. But again, when it comes to core values, the individual parts thread the fabric of the organizational culture. The organization's core values will always be less effective if they are not fueled by the known personal values of each and every individual in the organization.

Both personal and organizational core values are in motion. This is true regardless of the direction of the flow of values, needs, wants, and behaviors we previously discussed. Attention to neither, or to one without the other, impacts their powerful influence on this flow.

It will either be unintentionally driven by reaction or intentionally driven by response. Let's explore this subtle yet impactful nuance.

There are two predicable scenarios organizations can count on as they begin this process:

1. Most people won't know their own personal core values. Again, are they values-based? Likely. Do they have a gut feeling or intuition? Possibly. Do they have a grasp of the specifics? Rarely.

2. Most people would much rather discuss organizational core values than think about their own personal core values.

The first scenario has a whole lot to do with the reason for the second. I have come to realize there is another very human factor at play here.

When it comes to solely having organizational core values, we *react* to them. They're still outside us. We can hold them up and look at them, cognitively judge them, and, most conveniently, judge others with them. People often wait and see if others, especially those on the executive team, live these organizational values. If they do, then maybe they'll think about living them too. Unfortunately, few give the organizational core values much thought at all.

It isn't just that personal values have not been made part of the equation. While it's true most people don't know the specifics of their personal core values or have never been challenged to discover and put them into organizational play, most can't tell you the specific values of their organization, either.

There's a very cost-effective way to test this premise. Remember? It's called a blank sheet of paper!

If the organization's core values are known, they are often put forth and used as an inconsistent method of enforcement or compliance. In that sense, organizational core values can make for strong tools—even weapons—of judgment. As with gossip, it's surely easier (and a lot more fun!) when we can use organizational core values as a measurement stick against others. And when intentional personal core values are not in play, it's a lot more likely that this will happen.

For other organizations, that may not be their experience at all. They fall into the trap of making values the exception by honoring the living of organizational values in grand ways.

They may have wonderful awards of recognition at quarterly meetings for employees who have displayed an example of a behavior that demonstrates an organizational value. That, in itself, ought to be our biggest red flag—that living organizational core values is such a unique event that it deserves an award when it actually happens.

The absence of a personal connection to organizational core values makes it an exceptional practice. There is a reason for this. Because when organizational core values are outside of us, we will naturally *react* to them. Reactions tend to be situational rather than transformational. Ethics training and case studies only reinforce a situational application of values being a description of what we do rather than who we are. While it's a good practice to invest in as an insurance policy, it furthers a situational and reactionary mindset. Often the discussions and conclusions of such exercises draw on gut reactions rather than intentional connections to a list of organizational core values that most can't remember.

Personal core values are different. When we do the hard work of digging for them, discerning them, investigating them, test-driving them, claiming them, and finally owning them, we *respond* to them. We have discovered them, we have come to know them, we have embraced them, and now we own them. They are inside us. The natural flow of who we are becomes a response rather than a situational reaction. This alone changes everything.

THE NATURAL FLOW OF
WHO WE ARE BECOMES A
RESPONSE RATHER THAN
A SITUATIONAL REACTION.

It begins with the challenging yet refreshing work of identifying our personal core values. Once we have genuinely connected with our personal core values and understood the authentic value they can bring, it's natural for us to be drawn with interest to the core values of others. Not to judge them, but to know them and understand them.

It is genuine interest such as this that builds meaningful connections and genuine collaboration and shines a light on the deeper common ground of a diverse and multigenerational workforce. It is the ultimate team-building exercise where no outdoor adventure is needed, although such an adventure would be meaningfully enhanced if personal and organizational core values went along for the ride.

It's with this understanding of our personal core values and a connection to the core values of others that we begin to see organizational core values through a completely different lens. I have challenged thousands to do the hard work of discovering their own personal core values and then to look at the stated core values of their organization through the lens of their personal core values.

I then ask them to test my premise. I suggest that by looking through the clear lens of their personal core values they will see the organizational values in a richer way than they have ever seen them before.

Through this lens, they will find the insight to personally own the organizational core values. It is at this intentional intersection that we take the organizational core values, created on the outside, and bring them to our inside. It is here we begin to *respond* to personal and organizational core values alike and no longer merely react to either.

It is at this intersection—this connection—that an organization provides the opportunity for employees to know, understand, own, and hold themselves and then others accountable to the organizational core values. This is the intersection where natural alignment is seated and the reality of integrity is fueled. It's the integration of the two sets of core values that sparks authentic engagement.

When everyone engages in this process, we see the concept of shared values begin to emerge and be understood. This is not a set of values diluted in the mix of all the values pooled together. It is, rather, a strong current flowing in the right direction, fully engulfing the diversity of strong personal values and bringing to life the organizational values in lots of unique ways. Through the lens of their own personal core values, each individual engages in how they uniquely can bring each organizational core value to life every day.

Recently, a very successful professional asked me a question that seems to surface periodically when someone is starting to dig for their personal core values: "What if I discover my values don't align with my organization or my career?"

It's a logical question, and I'm sure there are some examples where the digging reveals a complete disconnect. In those cases, it sure seems like it would be a valuable confirmation of what I'm pretty certain the digger already knows! When there is no intersection and no one acts on it, everyone loses.

In most cases, however, the question begins with a false assumption of values being about where you are. Values point to who you are regardless of your whereabouts. Knowing your own core values and then taking the ownership to plug those values into bringing your organization's values to life each day could very well help you realize you are precisely where you need to be.

Remember, there are three other columns on your worksheet—needs, wants, and behaviors. If those elements are not fueled by an intentional set of core values, each is left more vulnerable to drift. Your needs, wants, and behaviors can misinform all that you see, what you experience, and how you respond to wherever you are. French-born novelist Anaïs Nin described the potential of this transformation quite well when she said, "We don't see things as they are, we see them as we are." It's so very true. When we know and then live from our true core, we will be amazed what can come about regardless of our whereabouts!

For the majority who discover the intersection of their personal and organizational core values, trust naturally surfaces into the mix of this flowing current. But none of this happens unless we first do the hard work of digging for and identifying our personal core values. It's hard to know others when you don't know yourself. It's easier to trust others when they know themselves and you know who they know themselves to be.

WHEN THERE IS
NO INTERSECTION
AND NO ONE ACTS ON IT,
EVERYONE LOSES.

THE VALUE OF CORE VALUES

How much value core values deliver in the end is in direct proportion to how much each individual values them from the beginning.

When I started becoming laser-focused on core values as a part of my overall writing and speaking on leadership, I quickly came to a sobering realization: We don't really value core values that much in business. I know this seems a bit harsh, but it also seems there are a number of other things we have come to really value in business much more: strategy, vision, mission, measurements, metrics, skills, and behaviors, among many other things. We might talk about how core values are important to have, but I'm talking about really valuing them.

We really value all these other things. We've talked about them frequently. We've referenced them constantly, measured them regularly, and held them high. They've been used as a mantra. They've almost been used as a theology all their own—with their own commandments, of sorts.

This led me to wonder if we truly understood the value of core values. It led me to believe that we needed to investigate the whole idea. It's hard to value something if you don't really know whether it actually brings value.

I proposed that for anyone to truly value core values, they first had to investigate and answer a very simple but defining question: Do you believe values build value? I suggest it's important for the investigation to precede the answer. I'm not looking for

HOW MUCH VALUE
CORE VALUES DELIVER IN
THE END IS IN DIRECT
PROPORTION TO HOW MUCH
EACH INDIVIDUAL VALUES
THEM FROM THE BEGINNING.

an immediate, gut-feeling answer to the question. I'm looking for an informed, well-thought-out, intellectual and emotional decision—for the kind of answer you could stand by, live for, and find value within.

I invite you to take on thirty days of investigation and introspection. Use every ounce of cognitive and analytical ability you can muster to determine whether core values add real value to business or not. I encourage you to draw on prior experiences as reference points, using real-life examples. Most importantly, I ask you to notice over the next thirty days (in meetings, challenges, decisions, and relationships) whether core values might make a difference and whether they can bring real value in every aspect of your work life.

I'm not looking for you to come to a right answer. I'm looking for you to make a decision. Let this same question wash over you at least once a day, every day, for those thirty days: Do I believe values build value? I request that for thirty days the answer simply be, "maybe." Maybe they do and maybe they don't. I then want you to come to one of two answers on the thirty-first day: yes or no. You need to be willing to own whatever answer you chose, because your answer will own you.

It's a great question to ponder as you are busy digging for your own core values. It is a question deserving of both intellectual and emotional analysis.

THE ALIGNMENT, ENGAGEMENT, AND SERVICE OF INTEGRITY

Depending on their size, organizations spend hundreds, thousands, or even millions of dollars in three distinct areas: alignment, engagement, and service. There is little argument among high-performing executives that each of these three areas will make an impact on the bottom line. Most would agree there is a return on investment that comes from investing in these areas. They may not agree on how much return, but most would agree there is a return. I don't know of any executive who would honestly desire misalignment, disengaged employees, or a continuous delivery of bad service to their customers, clients, or patients. This is why hundreds, thousands, or millions of dollars are invested. Unfortunately, these huge amounts are often invested in the wrong way.

I'm not a big fan of silk flowers; I prefer the real thing. Our neighbors across the street have the most beautiful gardens. Every spring, summer, and fall, their gardens are filled with an ever-changing variety of the real thing. There is not a silk flower in sight—because they don't invest in silk flowers. They invest in bulbs and seeds. They garden with care, and they receive an incredible garden.

We invest an awful lot of resources in expensive "silk flowers," and what we get is the artificial version of the real thing—artificial alignment, artificial engagement, and artificial service. We invest with good intentions, but we do so in the wrong way. We sell out when we could be cultivating and harvesting the real thing. The last time I checked, the "real thing" is always valued at a whole lot more than the artificial.

Intentionally discovered personal and organizational core values are the bulbs and seeds. You won't get silk flowers from them. Over time you will receive natural alignment, authentic engagement, and genuine service.

When we think of organizational alignment, we are most often referring to alignment with a vision, mission, strategy, and goals. It's about finding out if everyone is on the same page and getting aligned. Alignment is a good thing, but how you get people there vs. how people arrive there are two very different value propositions.

Silk flower alignment cultivates false positioning and posturing, spinning of stories and measurements, and—worst of all—meeting after the meeting. Looking like a flower and being a flower are very different things. Looking aligned and being aligned are two significantly different value propositions. It's about moving from honoring the call to get aligned to honestly being aligned.

Alignment doesn't begin with vision, mission, strategy, or measurements. At least, *natural* alignment doesn't begin there. It begins with the alignment of personal and organizational core values. If those values are in alignment and in play, there is a natural alignment that evolves from there. This critical alignment of values provides the context to see where there is misalignment between organizational core values and the mission, vision, and measurements of the organization. When those organizational values are known and intentionally lived every day, there is also clarity in which to see when mission, vision, and measurements are creating a drift away from those values.

The essence and intentional wording of the organizational core values give a common language with which to discuss any misalignment. Those same core values also provide the courage to have a discussion with anyone, at any time, regarding a perceived misalignment within the organization.

More importantly, the essence and intentional wording of the organizational values give the common language to intentionally create mission, vision, and measurements that are aligned in the first place.

Once personal and organizational core values are aligned, efforts can go into being sure the mission, vision, and measurements stay aligned with the values. When they do, you are nurturing *authentic* engagement.

We treat engagement as a choice—as a decision. We can make a choice to temporarily engage, and we create circumstances that will temporarily engage others. The problem is that it is only temporary, and temporary is like going to buy a silk flower arrangement of engagement. There is only one brand of authentic engagement. It's the engagement found at the intentional intersection of personal and organizational core values.

THERE IS ONLY ONE BRAND
OF AUTHENTIC ENGAGEMENT.
IT'S THE ENGAGEMENT
FOUND AT THE INTENTIONAL
INTERSECTION OF PERSONAL
AND ORGANIZATIONAL
CORE VALUES.

And then there is the experience of service. Service is not a methodology. Service methodologies work well for machines. A mechanical form of service works well in an ATM or on a well-thought-out website. But it doesn't work well for humans unless, of course, you want to turn them into robots, which is precisely what we have done to "service" in many organizations. We have streamlined and time-lined the service proposition. There is nothing genuine about it. Efficient on the surface? Maybe. Effective? Rarely. I call this "servicizing"—the mechanical form of service.

I'm amazed at how much we notice a genuine moment of great service. Some can't remember the last time they received genuine service because it's been so long. Others remember it clearly because it's so rare.

Genuine service is not a process. It's an expression of both personal and organizational core values. Genuine service is not a duty; it is an opportunity. It's not a commodity; it's a connection.

Ironically, the person served most by providing genuine service is the person providing the service, because it nourishes a deeper sense of authentic engagement. It becomes quite a systematic and synergistic process.

Silk flower alignment and silk flower engagement are empty enough. But there is nothing more slick or empty than silk flower service. There is nothing valuable or genuine about it. There is only one thing that creates and provides genuine service: core values.

SETTING THE BAR

During the period when I was writing the manuscript for *Return On Integrity: The New Definition of ROI and Why Leaders Need to Know It*, I was asked a number of questions to which I had no answer. It comes with the territory when trying to explore old concepts in fresh new ways.

Following the publication of the book, I anticipated—and eventually desired—that these kinds of questions would not only continue but increase. For these questions surface from a reader's engagement. Questions are not always in search of answers. If you allow them, they are an invitation to exploration and reflection. Recently, I was asked one of these questions toward the end of my presentation: "Who gets to set the bar on integrity?"

It's a great question, and one that is far more in search of exploration than explanation. It could also be an unintended search for an easy solution to an otherwise far more adventurous insight to integrity.

Setting a bar for integrity has more to do with compliance than realizing the full potential of core values. In other words, if someone can just tell us the standard to meet, then integrity becomes just another measure of our performance. This is not to say that compliance is not important; it has its place. It just should not be confused with integrity. Compliance can be a great data point and provide some wonderful teachable moments. Yet integrity is something different.

SETTING A BAR FOR
INTEGRITY HAS MORE TO
DO WITH COMPLIANCE
THAN REALIZING THE FULL
POTENTIAL OF CORE VALUES.

There are three words that surface within the definition of integrity that can be quite useful: "whole," "entire," and "undiminished."

You might think of this as "integrated." Integrity is not a measuring stick (or bar); it is a state of being, a condition. Rather than being measured from without, it is created from within. Outward signs of measurement do little for us without intentionally connecting to an inner compass.

You might also think of this integrated state of being as a state of flow. Psychologist Mihaly Csikszentmihalyi of the University of Chicago established the importance of flow in his best-selling book by the same title. I would suggest that flow is established when we are in a state of integrity, when all is integrated. This is true individually, and it is just as true collectively in an organization. An individual not in this state of flow can become a clot in the collective flow of an organization.

In an organization, the individual flow has to converge into a collective flow of shared organizational values. It is not possible to think of this individual flow or collective flow as separate from each other. They are intrinsically connected for as long as they are together.

The bar for integrity is not determined from without. When each individual takes ownership for digging to their own core values and embracing a well-established set of organizational core values, it is discovered from within and flows out from there.

BEING REALLY IN THE KNOW

Last week, I was on a first-time call with a new connection. Well into the call, he randomly asked me how I knew one of my LinkedIn connections. Fortunately, out of my hundreds of connections, he asked about one whom I know well. We aren't just connected; we *know* each other. If words matter, you might say that LinkedIn picked the right word; "connections" is a good description. Facebook on the other hand, in using the term "friends," made a bit of a stretch. That same stretch may well be at play when it comes to our core values. To say that you know your core values may be a bit of a stretch, too—even if you can list them.

This has made me realize how I've been underestimating the full meaning of the word "know" in my work on core values. I can't begin to recall each of the hundreds of times I've said, "Most people do not know their core values." The statement is true. Precisely what I'd been trying to say is that most people couldn't *list* their core values. In other words, most people can't specifically name them on a blank sheet of paper.

Most people consider themselves values-based, or they have a gut feel or intuition about their core values. For them, being able to identify/name their core values is a big step forward. It's hard to live what you can't identify. Yet being able to identify them is not enough. In fact, for many, it feeds a false assumption: If I can list them, I know them.

When asked about my LinkedIn connection, I really did know the person. We have shared common experiences—both good and bad—together. We have engaged in meaningful conversations, and we trust each other. There are other LinkedIn connections whom I know even better, based on even more common experiences and much deeper conversations. And then there are others in my LinkedIn account with whom I simply appreciate being connected. I trust that you can relate via your own social media accounts.

The process of getting to know your core values starts with a thoughtful exploration: an intellectual brainstorm mixed with a fair amount of silence and discernment. In fact, you likely will develop numerous drafts of lists in attempting to identify your core values, lists that include behaviors, wants, needs, and values. Over time, you will narrow each list and eventually make a claim of what you think are words that identify your core values.

At that point, you can celebrate for having identified them. It's a really important step forward. But it will be way too early to claim that you *know* them. In so many ways, at this point, you have just met them.

Knowing your core values is realized through the connection you develop with them, through living with them, and through being a student of them—taking them into your current life conditions and your day-in and day-out experiences. It is through these daily common experiences with them and nightly reflections upon them that you get to know them. Your needs, wants, and behaviors will be transformed by them. However, unlike a skill or behavior, the goal is not to *get better at* your core values.

It is about developing a *meaningful relationship with* them. You get to know them, and they get to know you.

As you get to know each other better, you will be surprised how much more valuable each of your core values becomes than the word you initially put on your list to best name them. Just because you know someone's name doesn't mean you know the person. The same is true with your values. As I have stated: "In your search for core values, you won't find them. They will find you!" I suppose the whole truth is that you find each other, and in doing so, you might say, you become great friends.

STAGECOACH JOURNEY

My friend Marianne used to quote her grandfather as saying, "Nothing truly great happens quickly." It's insightful wisdom that has stayed with me for over two decades. It may also explain why most stop short or settle for less.

In a world of rapid change and an obsession with the short term, this quote seems to run counter-culturally. When you combine this with the desire for immediate answers or "silver bullet" solutions, the essence of both patience and persistence get thrown out the window—and so does the possibility of greatness.

I have found this particularly true when it comes to one's exploration of their core values, whether it's a group of leaders investigating an organization's core values or an individual discovering their own. This process of discovery is, in fact, a trying exploration. It's more like taking a stagecoach, rather than a jet, to your destination.

When challenged to name our core values, many find it unsettling to simply start with a blank sheet of paper. Initially grasping for words and concepts can seem daunting. Most would prefer to be given a list of thirty words and pick a few that seem to resonate. I get that, and I could easily fall into the same desire to want to make it quick and easy. But quick rarely leads to what is great and almost never to what is true.

The discovery of our core is a bit of a wrestling match. It can get sloppy and confusing long before it gets clear and concise.

The wrestling, sloppiness, and confusion are what define the nature of our stagecoach journey.

In a world focused on efficiencies, one might rightfully ask: When a jet is available to get you to the destination, why in the world would you ever take a stagecoach? It's a really good question if greatness is defined by arriving at the destination. In discovering our core, greatness is created along the trail. The trail can be rough and sometimes the stagecoach will get stuck, and we will be forced to stop. In defining your core, I always recommend frequent stops along the trail. Work on it a while and put it away. Work on it some more and put it away. Eventually you arrive at a version 1.0 and you set up camp for a while and try it out, and then you find yourself working on it some more.

The conditions of the trail and the weather along the way are constantly changing as you slowly begin to discover what is stable within you.

When something is "easy" we tend to simply "use" it. But we ultimately "own" what we fully experience. The discovery of our core values is an experience to be owned. And core values only become valuable when we fully own them.

It's the natural struggle along the journey of the stagecoach ride that's the price of ownership. Picking a few words that resonate from a list of thirty options is like renting a house. No matter how many rent payments you make, you'll never own the house.

It is predictable and understandable that you will experience some level of values fatigue throughout this digging and discovery

IN DISCOVERING OUR CORE,
GREATNESS IS CREATED
ALONG THE TRAIL.

process. If, like most, you have never thought about personal and organizational core values this long or this deeply, hang in there. The stagecoach journey demands patience and persistence.

Patience and persistence pay the mortgage. The journey to the core can be a rough ride—getting stuck, confused, wanting to give up many times along the way—and is a normal part of the experience. In finding the will to keep going, we ultimately connect to our core.

It doesn't happen quickly, which is precisely why it can lead to greatness!

Pause Point

- As you continue to dig and discover, what are you seeing that is relevant and significant in your engagement, relationships, and serving others?

- On a continuum from being able to "list" your core values to "knowing" your core values, where are you at this point? What will be most difficult for your own patience and persistence along the stagecoach journey?

- At this point in your discovery, it would be helpful to revisit each of the questions of the previous Pause Points. As you review these questions, what new insights surface? How are your answers different than before?

Part Three

Destiny

Building traction, momentum,
and sustainability

Your return *to* integrity may appear sequential—dilemma, discovery, and destiny. It is, however, experienced more as a spiral, advancing ever deeper yet looping back around as it progresses. As you might surmise from your own earlier brainstorm of dilemmas, many of them will continue to exist whether you have discovered your core or not. Knowing your core values enables you to engage with those dilemmas in a more credible and valuable way. You will also find, through engaging with each dilemma, that your discovery continues to expand into ever-deepening insights.

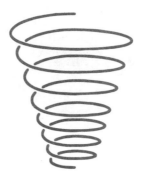

Destiny is not about your arrival at a destination. It might better be thought of as a doorway—as crossing the threshold to your way forward. Moment to moment. Day by day. This process is about effectiveness—embracing thoroughness, not speed. By this point, it is likely that you have thought more about core values, needs, wants, and behaviors than ever before. Yet, your way forward is just getting started.

At the same time, we have become conditioned to move on to the next new idea. In a world besieged by constant change, along with our ungrounded behaviors, wants, and needs massaged by branded one-liners, buzz-filled, flavor-of-the-month initiatives, and short attention spans, it may seem unnatural to sustain an intentional connection to our core. While this ongoing Destiny phase is designed for enhanced reinforcement, it may initially feel like an endless repetition. This repetition may very well create a sensation of values fatigue. Even if you don't experience this, others around you likely will and no doubt will encourage you to second-guess your own experience. When most have never consciously engaged a set of core values, it's not surprising that some might think of this as an exorbitant amount of focus on core values—especially by those who would rather do nothing about it at all.

It reprises the wisdom of an old management philosophy: The main thing is to keep the main thing, the main thing.

I find it fascinating that the entire composite of knowledge, resources, talent, and energy of some companies is invested in one product, which sometimes is just one part of what will become another company's product. Our day-to-day world functions because so many are laser-focused on their one product. This intense focus seems less consistent and more challenging when it comes to core values. It's easier to move on than to stay on the main thing—the one essential thing!

Wisdom is steadier than data. Data come and go. Ideas come and go. Issues come and go. Pet peeves come and go. Yet in a world of variety, the very important slow and steady have their way of creating the fatigue of sameness.

This sensation of values fatigue can catch you by surprise. Building a return on integrity in a culture that builds value with values actually requires a great deal of complexity and variety. It's like one prism constantly turning while reflecting a rapidly changing world around it. What you can experience is endless, yet your focus always returns to the one essential thing: the integrity of your core values.

I have no doubt that a battle of fatigue awaits anyone who embraces a commitment to build a return on integrity. You will certainly face this dilemma of values fatigue—until you learn to notice new things from the same stance.

PUTTING YOURSELF ON NOTICE

A beautiful Illinois prairie lies just a ten-minute walk from the front door of our home. Early last spring, the prairie's endless paths and undeniable convenience left me with little excuse from making a commitment to exercise several times a week by taking extended walks through the prairie.

Repeatedly putting on my running shoes to walk demanded its own new discipline. On most days, the initial ninety-minute walks tended to seem long as I dragged myself across the seeming sameness that blanketed the fields. The limestone pathways wound their way through green growth that most people would consider weeds in their own landscaped yards.

The commitment to walking kept me putting one foot in front of the other, week after week. The discipline itself became easier, and going for a walk soon felt more like a treat than a chore. It felt good, and I felt better each time I returned. I was months into this repetitive discipline when I stepped out my front door into a classic, 80-degree, sunny Chicago August afternoon. Fifteen minutes later, I was well on my way, mindlessly making strides across the assumed sameness. Then I realized the sameness had changed.

As my feet moved, my eyes shifted from one unique life form to another. I marveled at how the "weeds" had become a vivid bouquet of flowers. In the days and weeks to follow, the same path made its way through an ever-changing visual experience.

The same holds true when you open your eyes and notice what has been in front of you all along. In a world of electronic overload, we need fewer reminders, fewer notifications. Instead, we need to notice more. We need to notice the thing we've seen a thousand times—and see it again for the first time.

Recently, I was visiting with a friend. He shared the story of his younger brother who has lived on a tiny island for three decades. He had asked his brother if he ever got bored seeing the same thing day after day, year after year. His brother replied. "Every day I see something new." That's what happens when you notice.

When you put yourself on notice, clumps of weeds turn into bouquets, numb relationships evolve into friendships, and mundane experiences transform into adventures. After I put myself on notice, my walks and everything along them were never the same again.

Helen Keller's response, when asked if there was anything worse than being blind, was quite insightful: "Yes, being able to see and having no vision." When you put yourself on notice each and every day, you bring to life all five senses. You are able to experience the world in a new way. It's not the world that changes; it's you.

Therein lies everything you need to take the next step and clear the fog of an episode of values fatigue. Notice your core values in an ever-changing landscape. It's an important data point to understand before you begin the journey and one to keep in mind every step thereafter.

THE ULTIMATE ACCOUNTABILITY

Have you ever pondered something for an extended period of time, looking for some clarity only to have the answer find you in an unexpected moment? This happened to me while I was driving the roads of Chicagoland one crisp autumn afternoon.

For weeks, maybe months, I'd been contemplating why so many smart, well-intentioned people struggle with the concept of core values being the most strategic and untapped resource they have at their disposal. It had been especially puzzling to me, given that most everyone I had spoken with had confirmed their belief that core values were important. It felt like a disconnect.

It seemed like a fill-in-the-blank question, but it should have felt more like a multiple-choice question, one easy for me to answer. After all, I had written *Return On Integrity: The New Definition of ROI and Why Leaders Need to Know It*, which included various macro- and micro-dilemmas leaders must honestly face before being able to build value with core values. It would have felt appropriate to add the final multiple-choice option I had always hated on tests: all of the above.

While each dilemma I had written about seemed like a possible answer, the void I sensed seemed to keep driving toward a more appropriate choice: none of the above. I let this question of why so many struggle with the concept wash over me from time to time and from conversation to conversation. While I would brainstorm possible answers, nothing seemed to explain why a topic described as soft really seemed so hard.

I was stopped at a red light when the blank suddenly filled in for me. It was about accountability. Not just any accountability, the *ultimate accountability*. The kind of accountability that is very personal. The kind of accountability where you absolutely know where you stand. That is, if you've specifically defined your core. It's hard, however, to be accountable to a core left undiscovered. It's also easier to leave that core behind.

Nothing holds you more accountable than your core values. And that accountability can be hard. And frankly, within the everyday pressures in organizations—businesses, government, universities, sports programs, and churches—sometimes it can be quite inconvenient. It would seem that core values could demand from us in deeper and more personal ways than any other organizational measurement.

Accountability has its benefits—and its edge! This is especially true with ultimate accountability. It's not a monthly key performance indicator; rather it's a moment-to-moment monitor. If we are not careful, it can potentially feel punitive. The deeper we understand and embrace our values, the sharper the blade of accountability becomes. Who would want to sharpen that blade? In our human condition, no wonder an evasive resistance lurks within. Until, that is, you understand how to measure with grace.

Unlike most black-and-white organizational measurements, our accountability to an intentionally defined set of core values is measured in three-dimensional, living color. Our values aren't measured on paper or screens. They inform, guide, and transform

NOTHING HOLDS YOU
MORE ACCOUNTABLE THAN
YOUR CORE VALUES.

us through an ever-growing awareness within our mind, heart, and soul. And they do so when we measure ourselves and each other with a lot of grace.

Rather than beating you down, accountability builds you up. It doesn't measure what you do as much as how you do it. And in doing so, it defines the effectiveness of what you get done. That grace has a way of sharpening us beyond measurement.

DRIFT CATCHERS

While writing *Return On Integrity*, I was invited by a friend to speak to his leadership class of eighth-grade boys. It wasn't my typical corporate audience of executives, and I was a bit apprehensive whether these middle schoolers would find my message on core values interesting or relevant. I decided to share the quote on drift: "We don't go running away from our values, we go drifting away. And one day we wake up in a place we never meant to be, drifting in a direction we never would have chosen."

I wasn't prepared for the depth of their engagement or for the wisdom of one particular student in the closing question/answer session. He posed a thoughtful and brilliant question to which I was certain he had already figured out the answer. He said, "Mr. Blumberg, do you think other people see you drifting before you see it yourself?"

Better than waiting for others to notice your drifting is to proactively engage them to watch. I call them drift catchers. Given your permission, their gift is to call out your drift and encourage you back.

Catching our drift is very different from *getting* our drift. Oftentimes in the midst of drifting, we subconsciously want to explain it away to ourselves and to others. It's like the old saying we have used—you get my drift—when we're frustrated and want someone to understand what we are trying to explain.

You specifically give three things to your drift catchers:

1. A list of your personal core values;

2. A list of your organization's core values; and

3. The permission to tell you when they suspect or notice you're drifting from either list.

It's helpful to have at least one drift catcher inside your work-place and one outside. Depending on your circumstances, you may want more than one in either setting. Their different vantage points give you an added advantage.

The bottom line is that your drift catchers are those who love you enough to tell you the truth—*and I mean love exactly as I say it*—and you love them enough to accept their truth, even when you don't want to hear what they are saying. And if you share a mutual love, you will also be more likely to truly listen.

There is plenty of research and conventional wisdom that supports the value in going public with goals, ambitions, and resolutions. There is also great value in going public with your core values.

THE PM/AM EXAMINATION

Engaging your drift catchers is a valuable strategy for your destiny, but it still depends on others to respond to what they see in your behaviors and choices on the outside. Those behaviors and choices are also dependent on a sampling, because no matter who your drift catchers are, they are not with you 24/7. A second strategy is guaranteed to make the role of your drift catchers much easier. It is the PM/AM examination—as in, every evening and every morning.

The PM element of this strategy focuses on the reinforcement of your personal core values. Think "P" for personal. It's important that you keep this brief, because it's important that you keep it daily, seven days a week. The idea is simple. Each night, possibly as you are putting your head on your pillow, review the various scenes of your day through the eyes of your personal core values. Think about the beginning of your day and every person, meeting, challenge, and opportunity that followed. Review each one from three different vantage points:

1. Review those various scenes, noticing specifically where certain values came into play and really made a difference. It's important to notice where we get it right. This not only provides great encouragement and reinforcement, but we can learn how to become even more effective at bringing the noted value(s) to life in future situations.

2. Review those same scenes again, except this time look for where one of your values would have been helpful but you failed to draw on it. These are also great reminders and teachable moments that make us better the next time.

3. Finally, review your day in search of occasions where you might have violated one of your core values.

This is not a process designed so you will beat yourself up over a value you didn't engage or one that you specifically violated; you have a number of metrics and measurement tools you can use for that. This is primarily a tool of awareness—noticing where we either don't engage or violate a value, how we feel about it, and what insight can be gleaned for future reference. Each of these reviews can hold great wisdom for continuing to sharpen and strengthen your connection to your personal core.

The specific timing of this self-examination—just before falling asleep—is intentional. You will continue to process your awareness and related insights as you sleep. There is much published scientific research on the active and important functioning of the brain while we sleep. This research suggests that when you fall asleep the brain wakes up to do its most important functions of processing and sorting. You might as well have it working on your core values too!

The AM segment of this two-part technique focuses on the organizational core values. Think of the "A" as all of us. This review allows you to be proactive in engaging the organizational core values. There is no doubt your schedule is busy, and you have a natural sense of urgency in the early morning hours to get things started. You will want to limit this exercise to no more than five to seven minutes. Regardless of how busy your schedule might be, anyone can spare a few minutes. This is especially true when these minutes have the potential to return a hundredfold throughout the day, if not more!

This part of the technique has two segments:

1. Take the list and short narrative description (as applicable) of each organizational core value. Review just one value and description per day. The consistent commitment to this practice will have a cumulative impact of eventually embracing the entire list of values in a consistent way.

2. Look at your calendar for the day. This is an effective planning process to do anyway, regardless of core values. The key here is to look at your schedule through the lens of the value you just reviewed and think how that value might play a positive impact on your scheduled items. Think in terms of the people involved in those activities, the relational challenges and investments, the topics involved, discussions to be had, and decisions to be made. How does the value upon which you are focused impact any and/or all of them? What specific behaviors might that value intentionally put into action?

Don't be fooled by the PM/AM examination's simple structure. It will be harder than you might think and more effective than you likely imagine. Its impact comes through your repetitive commitment to its simplicity.

It's valuable to dig your water well. The real value is when you return to your well each day to get the water.

HOLDING COURT

Engaging your drift catchers and regularly honoring a commitment to your PM/AM examination will bring great value to you. Both work wonders for self-awareness but make terrible tools when used for judgment—that is, naming yourself as the drift catcher for all and examining everyone else night and day. When it comes to values, judgment comes easy if you are not careful.

Core values don't like to be used, they like to be lived! Rather than holding court, values allow us to court others by our example.

Following one of my keynotes on *Return On Integrity*, a participant approached me with great enthusiasm. He seemed completely energized by the session and engaged in the process of discovering his personal core values. He had already given a good bit of thought to his list of values, but he rightfully admitted that he had a ways to go.

After talking about his commitment to his core values, he drifted to a judgmental assessment of his teammates. He began to complain, "If only they had the same commitment." His tone changed from positive to pessimistic. And then he posed this question: "How do you deal with people like that?"

Knowing that he was looking for some kind of behavioral roadmap for him to fix the team, I simply said, "I'm not sure. How would your core values answer that question?" He humbly smiled and said, "I got it. I got some work to do."

When frustrated and disappointed in the noticeable drift of others, it will be your own core values that will protect you

CORE VALUES DON'T LIKE
TO BE USED,
THEY LIKE TO BE LIVED!

from reactive behavior and guide you to a proactive and worthy response. Even when the response requires a difficult decision, your values guide how the decision is made and carried out.

I believe one of the great benefits of truly knowing your own core values is the natural progression from there to a natural interest in the core values of others—not to judge them but to better understand them. I would go so far to say that this understanding eventually evolves to a deeper sense of empathy with them.

HARMONY BEYOND ALIGNMENT

The auditorium was packed with high school band members from all over the country. I was there to speak at the request of my friend and fellow speaker, Fran Kick. It wasn't my typical audience, and for this particular session I was in the audience amongst this highly energized crowd. I don't remember the speaker's topic or one ounce of content from his presentation, but I will never forget the experience he created.

In the middle of his presentation he asked everyone to stand. I knew from my own session with this crowd that these high school band members were enthusiastically responsive to instructions. They immediately stood with a stir and without a second thought I fell right into formation with them.

The speaker then gave the simple instructions that we were all going to hum a song. He noted his selection of "Amazing Grace" because he assumed the tune would be familiar to most everyone. He instructed all to begin on the count of three. And began it did. The sound sweetly and vastly filled the entire auditorium. I thought, Nice! The speaker didn't agree. He sourly gave us about a three on a scale of ten. I internally disagreed, noting this was a band conference, not a chorus conference. Bands play instruments; choruses sing.

He then raised the bar by asking everyone to give it their best, and everyone obliged. I couldn't believe the exponential difference. I felt a chill run through me as the humming wound down. The speaker held for a significant pause. I was certain he had chills too. His smile gave away his pleasure—or so I thought. He said, "Better. I'd say a seven." I thought, a *seven?* Are you kidding me? That was a twelve on a scale of ten.

I knew a third attempt was coming. That time, he did more than raise the bar. I don't remember all he said over the next minute. Something about digging way down. He then took a long pause. I do remember his last eight words: "I want you to give it your everything." As I write this, I still get chills thinking about the humming of those first several bars. It was amazing! It was in that moment that harmony found its way in.

Moments later it felt as if angels began to descend upon us. As we finished, there was a longer silence than before. I was deeply hoping the speaker would give us a nine so we could do it again. After a pause, he said, "That, my friends, was a ten. That was your everything."

But it was more than that. It wasn't only our everything. It was our everyone, together. There was no competition, no war between the left side and the right side of the auditorium or the front side and the back side of the auditorium. No male or female or any other segmentation. No uniforms to differentiate or segregate. It was everyone together, and from that togetherness came the opportunity for harmony to shine through. And it most certainly did.

It truly is amazing what happens when everyone digs for their greatest everything, an everything that rests deep within your core, waiting to be sung. It delivers an amazing grace—integrity. There is indeed a great return.

Pause Point

- Have you decided on your drift catchers? If not, who might be best? If so, have you reached out to them yet? How can you best collaborate with your drift catchers to make the most of this connection for each of you?

- How have your initial PM/AM examinations been? How can you make them more useful day-to-day?

- As you think about a project, vision, or dream at work, how do your personal values that intersect into the values of your organization invite you to show up to create a more valuable impact?

Closing Thoughts

I was in front of a room of thirteen hundred accounting and finance majors. The title the conference organizers had suggested for my closing general session was "Unleashing Authentic Relationships." Integrity and intentionally knowing and living your core values were at the heart of the presentation. The closing I had planned, however, was never delivered. The night before, a question grabbed me and wouldn't let go.

As I came to the closing of my presentation, I took a deep breath and said: "Now, I hope a few things I shared will stir your thinking and inspire your action to unleash authentic relationships. Yet, I would gladly trade all of that if you would regularly do just one thing every night—lay your head on your pillow and simply ask yourself one question: How loving was I today?"

The silence in the room was deafening. I took another deep breath and slowly continued: "We have corrupted what *love* is.

We have romanticized it, sexualized it, and manipulated it in a lot of ways. I challenge you to rediscover it. If you want to unleash authentic relationships, authentic leadership, and meaningful success, love is all you need. And the process to unleash that love starts and continues with that nightly question: How loving was I today?"

I somewhat trusted that this analytical audience would sense a bit of accountability in this otherwise very soft question.

Numerous students gathered around me after the presentation. They wanted to talk about one thing—the final question of an unplanned closing.

Beyond authenticity, I am certain, it's the only question that ultimately nurtures greatness. And it is intentionally digging for our core values and living them personally and organizationally that will fuel a rich answer to that question each night.

These values will also empower you to love what you do and love who you get to do it with. You might say this love is your greatest return on integrity. That is an ROI worth investing in.

Acknowledgments

The further I travel this journey, the more difficult it becomes to adequately express my breadth of gratitude that grows ever deeper while stretching ever wider. This project is an expression of the systemic accumulation of awareness, guidance, challenges, resistance and encouragement I have received along the way. All who have been a part of each and sometimes all of these aspects have contributed to the words your read across these pages. There are far too many to name at this juncture, but they individually know who they are. Rather than name them here, I will personally remind them as our paths cross again.

In so many ways, this project has taken me full-circle back to my first book, *Silent Alarm*. It has brought me back to a focus on the individual—the only one who ever makes the greater whole possible. It has also brought me back to those individuals who made my very first book possible. Clint Greenleaf believes in the "long game" in relationships and I'm grateful that our long-standing relationship allowed us to reconnect on this project. Clint always leads with a "yes" that makes all things possible. Jay Hodges was my first editor and now my most recent with fourteen years in between. I am grateful for his patience and persistence that were both needed as his development outpaced mine over those many years. Sheila Parr and Thom Lemmons have made us all look better through their creative expression and attention to details.

Words can't capture the gratitude I have for the endless encouragement my family gives me every step of my way—my love for Cindy, Ryan, Kelly and Julie is deeply integrated into my heart and my core.

My gratitude is most widely extended to some whom I may never meet—those who read these pages while picking-up their shovel to dig their well. Should our paths cross along the way, I will certainly consider it to be a special blessing on that day.

Collectively
Continuing to Dig

A s more and more readers continue to dig, we collectively gain further insight into the value of core values. Please visit with us at www.BlumbergROI.com/TheBigDig to continue to learn and share.

Join John on *The Front Porch* the last Thursday of each month by subscribing to his blog or monthly newsletter at www.blumbergroi.com/blog.

About the Author

Simply put, John G. Blumberg is inspiring an integrity movement at the intersection of personal and organizational core values.

In 1996, John left behind a career he loved—a career that had taken him from CPA to worldwide recruiting responsibilities at Arthur Andersen. From there, he followed his dream as a professional speaker and has presented to audiences in ten countries spread over three continents.

Over the last two decades, John has evolved his initial focus on what leaders do to what fuels who they really are. Today, John walks alongside the top leaders of organizations who want to build their own return on integrity, and he shares his message on ROI to all who dare to explore the value of their own core.

He is also the author of *Silent Alarm: A Parable of Hope for Busy Professionals, GOOD to the CORE: Building Value with*

Values, and *Return On Integrity: The New Definition of ROI and Why Leaders Need to Know It.*

John lives in Naperville, Illinois, with his wife, Cindy, where they raised their three children, Ryan, Kelly, and Julie.